AMERICA'S PRISONS

OPPOSING VIEWPOINTS®

Other Books of Related Interest

Opposing Viewpoints Series

America's Victims	The Homeless
Chemical Dependency	Juvenile Crime
Child Abuse	The Legal System
Civil Liberties	Mental Illness
Crime and Criminals	Poverty
Criminal Justice	Race Relations
The Death Penalty	Sexual Violence
Drug Abuse	Violence
Gangs	War on Drugs

Current Controversies Series

Drug Trafficking
Family Violence
Gun Control
Police Brutality
Urban Terrorism
Violence Against Women
Youth Violence

At Issue Series

Domestic Violence
The Jury System
Legalizing Drugs
The Militia Movement
Policing the Police
Single-Parent Families

AMERICA'S PRISONS

OPPOSING VIEWPOINTS®

David L. Bender, *Publisher*

Bruno Leone, *Executive Editor*

Scott Barbour, *Managing Editor*

Brenda Stalcup, *Senior Editor*

Charles P. Cozic, *Book Editor*

OPPOSING
VIEWPOINTS®
SERIES

Greenhaven Press, Inc., San Diego, California

Cover photo: Photodisc

Library of Congress Cataloging-in-Publication Data

America's prisons : opposing viewpoints / Charles P. Cozic, book editor.
  p.   cm. — (Opposing viewpoints series)
  Includes bibliographical references and index.
  ISBN 1-56510-550-8 (lib. bdg. : alk. paper). —
ISBN 1-56510-549-4 (pbk. : alk. paper)
  1. Prisons—United States. 2. Imprisonment—United States.
3. Alternatives to imprisonment—United States. 4. Criminals—
Rehabilitation—United States. I. Cozic, Charles P., 1957–   .
II. Series: Opposing viewpoints series (Unnumbered)
HV9471.A49 1997
365'.973—dc21   96-47990
                                                                      CIP

Greenhaven Press, Inc., P.O. Box 289009
San Diego, CA 92198-9009

"Congress shall make no law...abridging the freedom of speech, or of the press."

First Amendment to the U.S. Constitution

The basic foundation of our democracy is the First Amendment guarantee of freedom of expression. The Opposing Viewpoints Series is dedicated to the concept of this basic freedom and the idea that it is more important to practice it than to enshrine it.

CONTENTS

WHY CONSIDER
OPPOSING VIEWPOINTS?

"The only way in which a human being can make some
approach to knowing the whole of a subject is by hearing
what can be said about it by persons of every variety of
opinion and studying all modes in which it can be looked
at by every character of mind. No wise man ever acquired
his wisdom in any mode but this."

John Stuart Mill

In our media-intensive culture it is not difficult to find differing
opinions. Thousands of newspapers and magazines and dozens
of radio and television talk shows resound with differing points
of view. The difficulty lies in deciding which opinion to agree
with and which "experts" seem the most credible. The more in-
undated we become with differing opinions and claims, the
more essential it is to hone critical reading and thinking skills to
evaluate these ideas. Opposing Viewpoints books address this
problem directly by presenting stimulating debates that can be
used to enhance and teach these skills. The varied opinions con-
tained in each book examine many different aspects of a single
issue. While examining these conveniently edited opposing
views, readers can develop critical thinking skills such as the
ability to compare and contrast authors' credibility, facts, argu-
mentation styles, use of persuasive techniques, and other stylis-
tic tools. In short, the Opposing Viewpoints Series is an ideal
way to attain the higher-level thinking and reading skills so essential in a culture of diverse and contradictory opinions.

In addition to providing a tool for critical thinking, Opposing
Viewpoints books challenge readers to question their own
strongly held opinions and assumptions. Most people form their
opinions on the basis of upbringing, peer pressure, and personal, cultural, or professional bias. By reading carefully bal-
anced opposing views, readers must directly confront new ideas
as well as the opinions of those with whom they disagree. This
is not to simplistically argue that everyone who reads opposing
views will—or should—change his or her opinion. Instead, the

series enhances readers' understanding of their own views by encouraging confrontation with opposing ideas. Careful examination of others' views can lead to the readers' understanding of the logical inconsistencies in their own opinions, perspective on why they hold an opinion, and the consideration of the possibility that their opinion requires further evaluation.

EVALUATING OTHER OPINIONS

To ensure that this type of examination occurs, Opposing Viewpoints books present all types of opinions. Prominent spokespeople on different sides of each issue as well as well-known professionals from many disciplines challenge the reader. An additional goal of the series is to provide a forum for other, less known, or even unpopular viewpoints. The opinion of an ordinary person who has had to make the decision to cut off life support from a terminally ill relative, for example, may be just as valuable and provide just as much insight as a medical ethicist's professional opinion. The editors have two additional purposes in including these less known views. One, the editors encourage readers to respect others' opinions—even when not enhanced by professional credibility. It is only by reading or listening to and objectively evaluating others' ideas that one can determine whether they are worthy of consideration. Two, the inclusion of such viewpoints encourages the important critical thinking skill of objectively evaluating an author's credentials and bias. This evaluation will illuminate an author's reasons for taking a particular stance on an issue and will aid in readers' evaluation of the author's ideas.

As series editors of the Opposing Viewpoints Series, it is our hope that these books will give readers a deeper understanding of the issues debated and an appreciation of the complexity of even seemingly simple issues when good and honest people disagree. This awareness is particularly important in a democratic society such as ours in which people enter into public debate to determine the common good. Those with whom one disagrees should not be regarded as enemies but rather as people whose views deserve careful examination and may shed light on one's own.

Thomas Jefferson once said that "difference of opinion leads to inquiry, and inquiry to truth." Jefferson, a broadly educated man, argued that "if a nation expects to be ignorant and free . . . it expects what never was and never will be." As individuals and as a nation, it is imperative that we consider the opinions of others and examine them with skill and discernment. The Opposing Viewpoints Series is intended to help readers achieve this goal.

David L. Bender & Bruno Leone,
Series Editors

INTRODUCTION

"Building more prisons to address crime is like building more graveyards to address a fatal disease."

Robert Gangi, Time, February 7, 1994

"If we have overcrowded schools, we build more schools; it's the same for prisons."

Paul Kamenar, CQ Researcher, February 4, 1994

In the United States, rampant crime and a growing public demand for harsher penalties have fueled a boom in prison construction. In 1996, for example, 123 state and federal prisons opened or were being built. Even with such expansion, many prisons still house far more inmates than their intended capacities. In fact, forty states and the District of Columbia have been mandated by courts to relieve prison overcrowding.

With the nation's state and federal prison population exceeding 1.5 million, many corrections officials face the dilemma of finding *any* available space. For example, some inmates in Georgia are housed in trailers, while New Jersey prisons have resorted to tents. Several states, including Colorado, Missouri, and Virginia, have had to transfer inmates to prisons with open space in other states.

The recent trend toward tougher laws is expected to put even more criminals behind bars for longer periods of time. With much public support, many states and the federal government have passed "three strikes" laws that automatically impose life sentences on three-time felons. Other sentences have been lengthened for certain types of crime, such as rape and drive-by shootings.

Concerned about increasingly high rates of violent crime and fed up with a "revolving door" criminal justice system, many Americans favor imprisoning criminals for longer terms. In the words of the Council on Crime in America, "Our first order of business must be *restraining* known, convicted, violent, and repeat criminals." Advocates of lengthening prison sentences cite studies that found that approximately two-thirds of offenders placed on parole or probation were arrested for additional crimes. Furthermore, as Wisconsin appeals court judge Ralph Adam Fine notes, more than 60 percent of prisoners are repeat offenders, two-thirds of whom commit their latest crime while on parole or probation. Virginian George Allen is one governor who supports building more prisons and who has approved eliminating parole for offenders in his state. He asserts, "There is simply no safer way for the state to protect its citizens from society's most dangerous members."

Many experts agree that building more prisons and giving criminals longer prison sentences are the best approaches to reducing crime and convincing criminals that they will receive harsh punishment. Such efforts, they assert, will deter crime and keep dangerous criminals behind bars. In the words of author and criminal justice expert Robert James Bidinotto: "Incapacitation is the only *certain* crime-reduction method: while locked up, a felon can't commit more crimes." Former U.S. attorney general William P. Barr adds, "The choice is clear: More prison space or more crime."

However, other Americans disagree that building more prisons and imposing stricter criminal sentences will effectively reduce crime. These critics argue that prison traumatizes inmates and turns many into hardened criminals. The longer offenders are locked up, opponents maintain, the greater the chance they will embrace the criminal lifestyle. Columnist George A. Kendall writes, "Prisons, as everyone knows, end up being schools of crime with the most vicious criminals making up the faculty. Such teachers have a free hand to corrupt less experienced and less hardened criminals." Kendall and other critics of the prison system assert that the policy of warehousing inmates and the lack of rehabilitation programs that could help prisoners become law-abiding citizens will prove detrimental to society in the long run.

Critics maintain that instead of prison construction, money should be spent on preventing individuals, particularly youths, from becoming criminals. Prevention measures, they contend, must include education; job training; proper parenting, nutrition, and health care; and drug treatment. In the words of Morton Feldman, executive vice president of the National Association of Chiefs of Police, "We must either accept the fact that prevention is an absolute necessity or prepare to build a large prison on every street corner in every large city." Many observers argue that prevention programs should target a growing population of at-risk juveniles. According to former Texas governor Ann W. Richards: "It would be a lot cheaper and better to help [teenagers] now than it would be to lock them up in ten or fifteen years."

Rapid prison expansion also diverts funds from rehabilitation efforts, opponents maintain. As many states allocate increased amounts of money to build and staff prisons and to house prisoners, critics argue, they cut back on funding for programs such as vocational training and college courses. Some commentators contend that prisoners are losing important educational opportunities. In 1994, for instance, Congress banned inmates from using Pell grants to pay for prison classes. Barry Krisberg, president of the National Council on Crime and Delinquency, asserts, "When you eliminate these programs, you are increasing the odds that criminals will re-offend."

Advocates of harsher punishment of criminals maintain that only tougher laws and longer prison sentences will reduce crime. Critics argue that adopting such measures will compound the problem of prison overcrowding and will have little impact on crime rates. *America's Prisons: Opposing Viewpoints* examines this issue and other questions regarding prisons and inmates in the following chapters: Are Prisons Effective? How Should Prisons Treat Inmates? Should Prisons Use Inmate Labor? What Are the Alternatives to Prison?

CHAPTER 1

ARE PRISONS
EFFECTIVE?

CHAPTER PREFACE

In recent years, the number of U.S. prisons and inmates has soared. According to an August 1995 U.S. Department of Justice report, America's jail and prison population has more than tripled since 1980. But the rapid construction of new facilities still has not adequately relieved prison overcrowding, many observers contend. Federal and state prisons now operate at up to 25 percent above capacity, incarcerating 1.5 million inmates.

According to some experts, America's packed prisons are symptomatic of a failed corrections system. John Burton, a former chairman of the California Assembly's Public Safety Committee, maintains, "By any measurement, our corrections program is an utter failure." Many observers criticize the fact that a large percentage of the prison population consists of nonviolent drug offenders. In the words of Los Angeles Times columnist Robert Scheer, "Hardly an experienced judge can be found who really believes that throwing drug users into jail accomplishes anything positive for the individual or society." Scheer and others argue that rather than being incarcerated, these offenders should be assigned to intensively supervised probation and community drug treatment programs.

However, proponents of a get-tough approach to crime note that the majority of prisoners are violent criminals rather than nonviolent drug offenders. They insist that harsh and mandatory sentencing is necessary to keep such criminals off the streets. Bill McCollum, chairman of the House of Representatives subcommittee on crime, contends, "If you can get these violent criminals to serve more time, you will inevitably reduce the violent crime rate. Anyone who is locked up will not commit a crime." Others, asserting that drug offenders should be imprisoned, cite a Council on Crime in America finding that 80 percent of federal and state drug offenders are drug traffickers with a history of repeated offenses.

The question of whether drug offenders are taking up valuable prison space that could be used for more dangerous criminals is just one part of the controversy over prison effectiveness. Whether the prison system operates properly and effectively to keep criminals off the streets is debated in the following chapter.

"The policy prescription seems clear:
Build as many prisons as necessary
to lock up society's criminals for as
long as their sentences mandate."

THE PRISON SYSTEM WORKS

The Washington Times

In the following viewpoint, the Washington Times argues that increased rates of incarceration have contributed to a reduction in crime. Furthermore, the Times contends that the annual cost of operating a prison cell is far less than the cost incurred by a single violent crime. The editors conclude that more prisons should be built so that criminals will serve out their full sentences. The Washington Times is a conservative daily newspaper published in Washington, D.C.

As you read, consider the following questions:

1. What is the "if-then" question that the Times refers to?
2. According to the National Institute of Justice, cited by the editors, what is the annual cost of crime?
3. How much of their sentences do violent offenders serve, according to the Times?

"The Costs of Crime and Punishment," Editorial, Washington Times, April 28, 1996. Reprinted by permission of The Washington Times Corporation.

Expensive new prisons, both federal and state, have been springing up across the country for the past two decades. And for good reason. Actually, it's for two good reasons. First, the crime rate has skyrocketed during this period. Violent crime (murder, rape, robbery and aggravated assault) increased from 482 per 100,000 inhabitants in 1975 to 716 in 1994. The incidence of violent crime soared from one million offenses in 1975 to nearly two million in 1993. Property crimes increased by two million per year since 1975, and, of course, the explosion of cocaine—first powder, then crack—and other drug offenses contributed their share of imprisoned felons.

Second, after its 1960s failed experiment with liberal sentencing standards for violent offenders, society has been imposing longer prison sentences on a higher percentage of its criminals. Between 1960 and 1970, the number of offenders imprisoned for every 1,000 violent-crime arrests declined by 43 percent. During the 1970s, this trend reversed itself, and in the 1980s, the rate of incarceration accelerated. In 1975, fewer than 250,000 felons were incarcerated in federal and state prisons. By 1994, more than one million were imprisoned. The rate of incarceration more than tripled.

VIOLENT CRIME HAS DECLINED

Confusing cause and effect—for example, failing to acknowledge that increases in the incarceration rate followed increases in the crime rate—critics have ceaselessly argued that imprisoning more offenders during the past 20 years has failed to reduce crime. In fact, while today's violent crime rate remains dramatically higher than it was 20 years ago, it has begun to decline, falling from its 1991 peak of 758 per 100,000 inhabitants to 716 in 1994. Moreover, critics fail to address the very important—but impossible to quantify—"if-then" question. To wit, if society had not quadrupled its prison population during the past two decades, then what would its crime rate be today?

While constructing, staffing and operating new prisons are indisputably expensive undertakings, a study titled "Victim Costs and Consequences: A New Look" demonstrates that annual prison costs represent a small fraction of the total costs that crime imposes on society. How small? According to the study's sponsor, the National Institute of Justice, the research branch of the Justice Department, prison costs (including parole and probation operations), which total about $40 billion annually, account for about 8 percent of society's annual crime costs, which the study estimates to be nearly $500 billion.

The study calculates not only the tangible costs of property loss, police work, legal fees, foregone income from lost work time and medical expenses, but it also quantifies the difficult-to-measure intangible costs, such as pain, suffering, mental care and the "lost quality of life" incurred by the victim's family. In the case of murder, the report estimates intangible costs of $1.9 million. For rape victims, the study estimates tangible "out-of-pocket" costs of $5,100 and intangible, "quality of life" costs exceeding $80,000.

IN FAVOR OF PRISONS

I have studied prisons all around the country. The vast majority protect inmates from each other, provide basic amenities, offer basic services and do so in a way that respects prisoners' basic constitutional and legal rights. Moreover, in the federal prison system, and in several state prison systems, prisoners receive better drug treatment than they could get on the streets. And, regardless of the conditions of confinement, all the data show that criminals who go to prison are far less likely to commit crimes in the future than otherwise comparable criminals who do not go to prison.

John J. DiIulio Jr., *Wall Street Journal*, May 13, 1992.

Once intangible costs are included, as they must be, it becomes clear that the $20,000–$25,000 annual cost of a prison cell is a relatively small price to pay to prevent the perpetration of a single violent crime, to say nothing of the multiple crimes committed by the typical repeat offender. Critics of the report have argued that its authors, who based their cost formula in part on the size of jury awards to crime victims and their families (which have been skyrocketing, as we all know), have thusly hyped their total. So what? Even if they overestimated intangibles by a factor of four, it is still clear that the benefits of prison construction far exceed their costs. In fact, a 1990 National Institute of Justice study found that the typical inmate, while pursuing his out-of-prison illegal activities, costs society between $172,000 and $2,364,000 per year. A 1982 RAND Corporation analysis put society's annual cost at $430,000 per year as a result of the criminal activity of released inmates.

Considering the utterly unacceptable costs of crime and the fact that Bureau of Justice statistics reveal that violent offenders are still serving less than half their original sentences, the policy prescription seems clear: Build as many prisons as necessary to lock up society's criminals for as long as their sentences mandate.

| "Our nation's moral jihad against crime is causing us to devour ourselves through perpetual, prolific prison-building."

THE PRISON SYSTEM DOES NOT WORK

Jon Marc Taylor

Despite massive spending on prison construction, Jon Marc Taylor argues in the following viewpoint, the level of crime has not dropped and most released prisoners eventually return to prison. Taylor maintains that America's prison systems violate inmates' human rights and fail to rehabilitate prisoners. He suggests that the money being spent on prisons would be more wisely invested in successful rehabilitation programs and in education. Taylor is a contributing editor for *Prison Life* magazine and an inmate at Jefferson City Correctional Center in Missouri.

As you read, consider the following questions:

1. According to Taylor, what percentage of prisoners return to prison?
2. Why do communities want to attract prison construction, according to the author?
3. In Taylor's opinion, how does society in the 1990s compare with society in the "dysfunctional '60s"?

Jon Marc Taylor, "Prison Economics 101," *North Coast XPress*, August/September 1996. Reprinted by permission of the author.

Our nation's moral jihad against crime is causing us to devour ourselves through perpetual, prolific prison-building. We have 1.1 million people imprisoned and another 500,000 jailed, yet we are historically no safer today—nor in any greater danger of harm—than we were a century ago.

Over the past fifteen years, government spending on prison construction has increased more than 600%, yet construction represents only 6% of a prison's total cost over its usable lifetime. The increases in both spending and appropriations in state corrections for 1996 have by far outpaced every other budget category. In 1980, correctional spending consumed only 1% of state spending, and that was thought huge at the time. Now prisons voraciously eat up 5% of the commonwealth's spending at the expense of everything and everyone else.

California once had a world-class, highly accessible public higher-education system that was the envy of the world. Now it ranks 46th in higher education funding. Along with Florida (both of which operate two of the largest penal systems in the world), Californians are spending more to incarcerate their citizens than to educate their children. Michigan is not far behind. Texas is dead last in public high school graduation rates—presently building more prisons than anyone else to house lawbreakers, 85% of whom are high school dropouts. States on average this fiscal year [1995–96] are increasing their investments in public and higher education by 5%, Medicaid by 7%, and Aid to Families with Dependent Children a paltry 6%, reserving a double-digit increase of 13% for corrections.

MORE SPENDING HAS NOT HELPED

Even with all this spending—tripling prison populations—the level of crime has essentially remained unchanged over the past twenty years. Yet office-holders predict dire perils ahead. This tremendous public investment, moreover, has not resulted in a better, more efficient, or humane system. Over 60% of those who go in and get out, eventually go back. Although the failure of rehabilitation programming is not the culprit, the lack of its investment is.

A comprehensive analysis of 443 studies on rehabilitation programs concluded that they do work when certain principles are followed. They demonstrate 10–50% or even greater reductions in recidivism, and subsequently in reduced victimization and expensive revolving reincarceration as well. Paradoxically, rehabilitation programs receive only crumbs from the prodigious correctional pie—less than five cents of every dollar.

Nor is it true that we have built the country club prisons so vocally derided by our statesmen and women. In fact, our nation's prison systems are in violation of the universal Declaration of Human Rights and the International Convention on Civil and Political Rights, with a European commission finding the U.S. penal archipelago to be the "most barbarous" of the western world. At home, as well, the courts have placed 39 states under orders or consent decrees to clean up their acts. Prisons don't affect crime rates, won't rehabilitate those incarcerated, and aren't palaces of luxury and leisure.

They are, on the other hand, public work projects "ninetiesstyle." Communities fiercely compete in prison derbies to attract a clink to their county. And why not! Hundreds of jobs deliver-

PRISON COSTS

ELEANOR MILL / MILL NEWSART SYNDICATE

Eleanor Mill. Reprinted by permission of Mill NewsArt Syndicate.

ing salaries and benefits averaging in the mid-$20,000s, the stimulating provision of sundry supplies, and a steady stream of visitors to buy gas, meals, and lodging, is the economic jackpot in an era of relocated factories, work force reductions, and shrinking real wages.

In the Golden State, the rainbow's reward is even greater, with standard guard pay-packages exceeding $55,000—tens of thousands more than school teachers. No wonder the operation of West Coast gulags is more appreciated than grade schools.

SOCIAL FOLLY

If we add the possible male work force currently incarcerated to present unemployment rates, those figures would jump nearly two points, closing on 9%. Some economists now worry that high incarceration levels will become a drag on future economic growth. When eventually released, these potential laborers lugging prison records, with poor education, little practical training, and deficient social skills, won't be of much economic value. So we continue spending more on prisons and less on schools, roads, and research. Crime keeps on victimizing as before. And we are buying a less capable, more alienated work force. Compared to our "dysfunctional '60s," we have wrought a less civilized, more economically and socially divided society.

Time marches on and we still build more prisons to putatively make our streets safer, while employing the laid-off corporate worker in a taxpayer-subsidized job at half his/her previous wage and, in turn, laying off the college professor, public health nurse, and social worker to fund further prison expansion. Ad infinitum; ad nauseam.

Historian Barbara Tuchman, analyzing self-destructiveness in declining civilizations, describes governmental folly as a policy that is perceived as counterproductive, but nevertheless is pursued anyway.

The next time a politician calls for more prisons, tougher jails, or ever more harsh terms, remember [philosopher] Friedrich Nietzche's dictum to distrust all in whom the urge to punish is strong. For they are punishing all of us with their folly.

| "We need to recognize that imprisonment offers ... social benefits."

IMPRISONMENT IS BENEFICIAL

Council on Crime in America

In the following viewpoint, the Council on Crime in America asserts that imprisonment benefits society in several ways. Imprisonment, the council contends, is a form of retribution that ensures the offender is punished and meets society's desire to see justice served. Prison programs aimed at rehabilitating offenders reduce the chances that they will commit other crimes upon release, the authors maintain. Furthermore, the authors argue, people are often deterred from committing crimes by the knowledge that they would be imprisoned if caught. According to the council, prisons also incapacitate dangerous criminals by removing them from society and placing them in prison, where they are unable to commit more crimes against the general public. The council is a program of the New Citizenship Project, a conservative public policy group in Washington, D.C.

As you read, consider the following questions:

1. Which of the four social benefits of imprisonment is easiest to measure, according to the council?
2. According to the council, how much does it cost society to incarcerate an offender for one year?
3. In the authors' opinion, what sentencing policies should the justice system adopt?

From "The States of Violent Crime in America," the First Report of the Council on Crime in America, January 1996. Reprinted by permission of the New Citizen Project, Washington, D.C. (Original footnotes have been omitted here).

W e continue to be amazed that many crime analysts and others refuse to acknowledge the data on how socially beneficial and cost-effective a crime-restraint tool imprisonment can be.

For example, many experts and commentators who must truly know better continue to assert that increased levels of incarceration have been a failure because increased imprisonment rates have not always been followed immediately by decreased crime rates. But as these same students of the subject are normally the first ones to emphasize, crime rates are largely a complex function of demographic and other variables over which the justice system, do whatever it will, can exercise relatively little direct control. As National Bureau of Economic Research economist Steven D. Levitt has observed, "To the extent that the underlying determinants of crime . . . have worsened over time, the increased use of prisons may simply be masking what would have been an even greater rise in criminal activity."

To state the point a bit more bluntly, it apparently takes a Ph.D. in criminology to doubt that if we released half of all prisoners tonight, we would experience more crime tomorrow. This common sense of the subject—the obvious reality that prisons restrain convicted criminals from committing large numbers of crimes that they would be committing if free—is supported not only by the empirical data on crime committed by community-based convicted criminals, but by a number of studies which estimate how much undetected and unpunished crime prisoners did before being taken off the streets.

FOUR TYPES OF BENEFITS

To begin, we need to recognize that imprisonment offers at least four types of social benefits. The first is retribution: imprisoning Peter punishes him and expresses society's desire to do justice. Second is deterrence: imprisoning Peter may deter him or Paul or both from committing crimes in the future. Third is rehabilitation: while behind bars, Peter may participate in drug treatment or other programs that reduce the chances that he will return to crime when free. Fourth is incapacitation: from his cell, Peter can't commit crimes against anyone save other prisoners, staff, or visitors.

At present, it is harder to measure the retribution, deterrence, or rehabilitation value of imprisonment to society than it is to measure its incapacitation value. The types of opinion surveys and data sets that would enable one to arrive at meaningful estimates of the first three social benefits of imprisonment simply do not yet exist. But it is possible to estimate how much serious crime is averted each year by keeping those convicted criminals who are sentenced to prison behind bars, as opposed to letting them out on the streets.

Based on large prisoner self-report surveys in two states (Wisconsin in 1990, New Jersey in 1993), two Brookings Institution studies found that state prisoners commit a median of 12 felonies in the year prior to their imprisonment excluding all drug crimes. Other recent studies offer higher estimates. For example, Steven D. Levitt has estimated that "[I]ncarcerating one additional prisoner reduces the number of crimes by approximately 13 per year, a number in close accordance with the level of criminal activity reported by the median prisoner in surveys." Likewise, William and Mary economists Thomas Marvell and Carlisle Moody have estimated that "in the 1970s and 1980s each additional state prisoner averted at least 17 [FBI] index crimes. . . . For several reasons, the real impact may be somewhat greater, and for recent years a better estimate may be 21 crimes averted per additional prisoner."

THE COSTS OF CRIME

Of course, it costs society as much as $25,000 to keep a convicted felon or repeat criminal locked up for a year. Every social expenditure imposes opportunity costs (a tax dollar spent on a prison is a tax dollar not spent on a preschool, and vice versa). But what does it cost crime victims, their families, friends, employers, and the rest of society to let a convicted criminal roam the streets in search of victims?

A recent study of the costs of crimes to victims found that in 1992 economic loss of some kind occurred in 71 percent of all personal crimes (rape, robbery, assault, personal theft) and 23 percent of all violent crimes (rape, robbery, assault). The study estimated that in 1992 crime victims lost $17.2 billion in direct costs (losses from property theft or damage, cash losses, medical expenses, lost pay from lost work). This estimate, however, did not include direct costs to victims that occurred six months or more after the crime (e.g., medical costs). Nor did it include decreased work productivity, less tangible costs of pain and suffering, increases to insurance premiums as a result of filing claims, costs incurred from moving as a result of victimization, and other indirect costs.

Another study took a somewhat more comprehensive view of the direct costs of crime and included some indirect costs of crime as well. The study estimated the costs and monetary value of lost quality of life in 1987 due to death and nonfatal physical and psychological injury resulting from violent crime. Using various measures, the study estimated that each murder costs $2.4 million, each rape $60,000, each arson $50,000, each assault $25,000, and each robbery $19,000. It estimated that lifetime costs for all violent crimes totaled $178 billion during 1987 to 1990.

Even these numbers, however, omit the sort of detailed cost accounting that is reflected in site-specific, crime-specific studies. For example, a survey of admissions to Wisconsin hospitals over a 41-month period found that 1,036 patients were admitted for gunshot wounds caused by assaults. Gunshot wound victims admitted during this period accumulated over $16 million in hospital bills, about $6.8 million of which was paid by taxes. Long-term costs rise far higher. For example, just one shotgun assault victim in this survey was likely to cost more than $5 million in lost income and medical expenses over the next 35 years.

Four Benefits

On average, it costs about $25,000 a year to keep a convicted criminal in prison. For that money, society gets four benefits: Imprisonment punishes offenders and expresses society's moral disapproval. It teaches felons and would-be felons a lesson: Do crime, do time. Prisoners get drug treatment and education. And, as the columnist Ben Wattenberg has noted, "A thug in prison can't shoot your sister."

All four benefits count. Increased incarceration explains part of the drop in crime in New York and other cities. As some studies show, prisons pay big dividends even if all they deliver is relief from the murder and mayhem that incarcerated felons would be committing if free.

John J. DiIulio Jr., *New York Times*, January 16, 1996.

How much of the human and financial toll of crime could be avoided by incarcerating violent and repeat criminals for all or most of their terms?

One study, commissioned by the National Institute of Justice, found that the "lowest estimate of the benefit of operating an additional prison cell for a year ($172,000) is over twice as high as the most extreme estimate of the cost of operating such a cell ($70,000). Likewise, the first Brookings study found that imprisoning 100 typical felons "costs $2.5 million, but leaving these criminals on the street costs $4.6 million." The second

Brookings study found that for every dollar it costs to keep the typical prisoner behind bars "society saves $2.80 in the social costs of crimes averted."

IMPRISONMENT PAYS OFF

And remember: these studies measure the social benefits of prisons solely in terms of imprisonment's incapacitation value. Because there is every reason to suppose that the retribution, deterrence, and rehabilitative values of imprisonment are each greater than zero—that is, because it is virtually certain that in addition to incapacitating criminals who would commit crimes when free, prison also succeeds in punishing, deterring, and rehabilitating at least some prisoners under some conditions—these estimates of the net social benefits of imprisonment are bound to be underestimates. And if, therefore, estimates made only in terms of prison's incapacitation value are positive, it means that the actual social benefits of imprisonment are even higher and that prison most definitely pays for the vast majority of all prisoners.

As if any further evidence were needed, we note that in 1989 there were an estimated 66,000 fewer rapes, 323,000 fewer robberies, 380,000 fewer assaults, and 3.3 million fewer burglaries attributable to the difference between the crime rates of 1973 versus those of 1989 (i.e., applying 1973 crime rates to the 1989 population). If only one-half or one-quarter of the reductions were the result of rising incarceration rates, "that would still leave prisons responsible for sizable reductions in crime," according to Patrick A. Langan. Tripling the prison population from 1975 to 1989 "potentially reduced reported and unreported violent crime by 10 to 15 percent below what it would have been, thereby potentially preventing a conservatively estimated 390,000 murders, rapes, robberies, and aggravated assaults in 1989 alone."

Still, it is important to caution that prison does not necessarily pay for each and every imprisoned felon. Moreover, the hidden costs of incarceration include losses in worker productivity and employability. Likewise, long-term imprisonment spells harmless geriatric inmates and associated health care costs. On the other hand, many incarcerated persons enter prison with anemic work records, a history of welfare dependence, and a fair probability of having to rely on government to pay for their health care whether or not they are incarcerated. And there are some geriatric prisoners whom we would want to remain in confinement purely for the sake of just desserts.

Also, while we know that prison pays, we do not know why per capita corrections spending varies so much from one jurisdiction to the next, why spending has risen so sharply in some places but not in others, or where the greatest opportunities for efficiency gains may lie. For example, prison operating costs in Texas grew from $91 million in 1980 to $1.84 billion in 1994, about a tenfold increase in real terms, while the state's prison population barely doubled. In Pennsylvania and other big states, corrections spending has grown much more slowly. Overall, Americans spend barely a penny of every tax dollar on prisons and jails. Thus, before Americans and their leaders can get a real policy-relevant handle on the social costs and benefits of incarceration versus other sentencing options, scholars will need to dig much deeper than criminologists have dug into the basic public finance questions related to crime and punishment.

For now, however, it is enough to acknowledge the overwhelming empirical evidence that, as the columnist Ben Wattenberg has quipped, "a thug in prison can't shoot your sister."

RESTRAINING VIOLENT CRIMINALS

In sum, the simple truth is that, relative to the millions of crimes, including violent crimes, that are committed each year in America, the justice system imprisons only a small fraction of all offenders, including only a small fraction of all violent offenders. Not surprisingly, therefore, those who really do go to prison in this country today are almost without exception the worst of the worst predatory career criminals. Not only are their official criminal records punctuated by many different types of serious crimes; they commit tremendous numbers of violent and other crimes that go wholly undetected, unprosecuted, and unpunished.

Scratch the criminal-records surface of most imprisoned "non-violent" prisoners, most "mere parole violators," and many "low-level drug offenders," and you will almost invariably find evidence of a life of crime that stretches back many years. These records, moreover, most likely include categories of offenses other than the ones for which the felon was most recently convicted, sentenced, and imprisoned. In addition, most imprisoned offenders, including the most violent ones, spend relatively little time behind bars before being released. For almost all of them, their conditions of confinement are quite humane. Problems of prison "overcrowding" are real but much exaggerated, and most prisoners enjoy access to a wide range of amenities and services behind bars.

Americans are paying a heavy human and financial toll for government's failure to restrain violent criminals, adult and juvenile. Given the country's crime demographics, and unless the system changes, over the next decade that toll is bound to become even heavier. Already the self-inflicted wound of serious crime done by persons on probation, parole, or pretrial release has begin to fester. Known offenders who are not restrained do as much as a third of all violent crime. Probationers and parolees are responsible for literally millions of crimes each year, including thousands of murders.

In our view, however, the answer is not to incarcerate every convicted felon, or even every convicted violent felon, for decades or for life. Nor is the answer to make conditions of confinement for those offenders who do end up behind bars harsh or inhumane; running "no-frills" prisons is not synonymous with curtailing revolving-door justice (although humane but spartan prisons certainly may have some deterrent effect). Going harder on the relatively small number of violent offenders in prison will do little to restrain the much larger (and younger, more impulsive, and harder to deter) violent offenders who roam free.

MORE EFFECTIVE CRIMINAL JUSTICE

Rather, our view is that America needs to put more violent and repeat criminals, adult and juvenile, behind bars longer, to see to it that truth-in-sentencing and such kindred laws as are presently on the books are fully and faithfully executed, and to begin reinventing probation and parole agencies in ways that will enable them to supervise their charges, enforce the law, and enhance public safety. If the justice system were operating effectively in the public interest, then the challenge of restraining violent criminals, adult and juvenile, would be met more aggressively by all levels of government.

Americans are entitled to an honest, realistic civic discourse about restraining violent criminals, adult and juvenile. Before such a discourse can proceed, however, it must become unacceptable in elite circles to deny, discount, or disparage the public's legitimate desire to slow or stop revolving-door justice. In the 1960's and 70's, prisoners' rights activists and anti-incarceration analysts called for moratoria on prison construction ("Tear down the walls!"). Today many of these same people, flanked by various national media commentators, are battling—sometimes openly, but as often behind the scenes—to eliminate mandatory minimum laws, abolish or subvert truth-in-sentencing laws, and block any species of three strikes laws. They freely publicize and propagandize about the social costs of incarceration while choking off public discussion of its considerable social benefits. They lobby to expand the capacity of activist judges to impose prison caps which trigger the release of dangerous felons. In short, they achieve through junk science, administrative discretion, or judicial fiat what could not be achieved through democratic debate and legislative action.

In our view, and at a minimum, those who continue to ignore or to trivialize the facts about crime and punishment in America should be required by the press, policymakers, and the people to be more specific. For example, those who continue to assert that America should not imprison low-level drug offenders should tell us who, precisely, is to count as a "low-level drug offender." Of the 241,709 new court commitments to thirty-five state prisons in 1991, 74,423 (30 percent) were convicted of drug law violations, 16,632 of them for possession, the remaining 55,791 for drug trafficking and related crimes. Of the 36,648 new court commitments to federal prisons in 1991, 14,564 (42 percent) were drug law violators, 703 (2 percent) were convicted of possession, the remaining 13,861 for drug trafficking and related crimes. Most imprisoned drug traffickers are hardly first-time felons or strictly small-time dealers; many have quite diversified criminal portfolios involving violent and property crimes as well as drug crimes. The average quantity of drugs involved in federal cocaine trafficking cases is 183 pounds, while the average for marijuana traffickers is 3.5 tons.

The truth about revolving-door justice and who really goes to prison is not pleasant. Acknowledging and acting on this truth will not set many violent or repeat prisoners free, but it will help to restore public trust and confidence in the justice system—and, over time, in representative government itself.

| "The increase in the prison population did not reduce crime, nor did it make Americans feel safer."

IMPRISONMENT IS NOT BENEFICIAL

National Criminal Justice Commission

The National Criminal Justice Commission is a project of the National Center on Institutions and Alternatives in Washington, D.C. In the following viewpoint, the commission argues that imprisonment does not benefit prisoners or reduce crime. The commission asserts that the dangerous prison environment traumatizes many inmates, endangers their personal safety, and increases their anger and rage toward society. In particular, the commission maintains, the practice of imprisoning small-time nonviolent offenders does little to rehabilitate criminals or to lower crime rates. Prison expansion also diverts funds from education and welfare, according to the authors.

As you read, consider the following questions:

1. According to experts cited by the commission, what do many young males find appealing about imprisonment?
2. To what does Joanne Page compare the impact of incarceration, according to the commission?
3. How much does California spend on prison construction annually, according to the authors?

Excerpts from *The Real War on Crime: The Report of the National Criminal Justice Commission*, Steven R. Donziger, ed. Copyright ©1996 by the National Center on Institutions and Alternatives. Reprinted by permission of HarperPerennial, a division of HarperCollins Publishers, Inc.

S ince 1980, the United States has engaged in the largest and most frenetic correctional buildup of any country in the history of the world. During this time the number of Americans imprisoned has tripled to 1.5 million. About 50 million criminal records—enough to cover nearly one-fifth of the entire U.S. population—are stuffed into police files. Hundreds of billions of dollars have poured from taxpayers' checking accounts into penal institutions and the businesses that service them. Several million people have come to depend on the criminal justice system for employment.

LESS MONEY, MORE CRIME

The hidden side of the growth of the criminal justice system is its direct effect on how much less money Americans spend on education, parks, libraries, recreation centers, highways, and universities. With a significant percentage of the potential male workforce in prison, our high rates of incarceration also act as a drag on economic growth. One estimate has the nation's jobless rate rising from 5.9 percent to 7.5 percent if male prisoners were counted as part of the labor force.

One would think that the extraordinary expansion of the criminal justice system would have made at least a small dent in the crime rate. The increase in the prison population did not reduce crime, nor did it make Americans feel safer. In fact, some criminologists have argued that the overuse of the penal system for so many small-time offenders has actually created more crime than it has prevented, a topic we will explore shortly. . . .

THE EFFECTS OF INCARCERATION

Anyone who has been handcuffed by police knows how deeply humiliating the experience can be. Imagine the effects of spending even a night in the bizarre and violent subculture of most jails. Literature abounds with examples of people traumatized by the experience. Each person booked is fingerprinted and photographed for their criminal record (the record remains with them even if the charges are later dropped). Basic survival tactics are necessary to endure even a short stay. Inmates learn to strike first and seek strength in gangs often comprised of dangerous offenders. Sexual assaults are frequent and usually go unpunished. The prison experience is one in which the code is survival of the fittest, in which weakness is a crime, and in which the expression of vulnerable feelings can jeopardize the survival of the prisoner. As ever more young men and women are socialized to the cell blocks and then are returned to the streets, the violent subculture of the correctional facility increasingly acts as a vector for spreading crime in our communities. Prisons and jails thus have a dual effect: They protect society from criminals, but they also contribute to crime by transferring their violent subculture to our community once inmates are released.

In many communities, spending time locked up is such a natural part of life that correctional facilities have lost their ability to scare people into good behavior. In California, 40 percent of youths in custody have a parent who has done time. Experts on the inner city point out that many young men do not mind going to prison because they see it as a glamorous rite of passage that earns respect and status. The New York Times described a scene on the South Side of Chicago where neighborhood youth surrounded an ex-inmate who came home "as if he were a rap star passing out concert tickets."

FEAR AND ANGER

Commission member Joanne Page has worked with ex-offenders for years as the director of The Fortune Society in New York City. She compares the impact of incarceration to post-traumatic stress disorder, which often afflicts soldiers who return home from war. Many offenders emerge from prison afraid to trust, fearful of the unknown, and with their vision of the world shaped by the meaning that behaviors have in the prison context. For a recently released prisoner, experiences like being jostled on the subway, having someone reach across them in the bathroom to take a paper towel, or staring can be taken as the precursor to a physical attack. Professionals who work with ex-offenders have said it appears prison damages a person's midrange response to the environment, leaving the choice of gritting one's teeth and enduring, or full-fledged attack to protect oneself from perceived danger. In a relationship with a loved one, this socialization means that problems will not easily be talked through, but are more likely to result in a blowup or an absence of communication. In a job situation, this means tensions are more likely to result in a loss of temper or in the failure to show up for work.

JAIL AND PRISON CONDITIONS

A few elected officials have sought to rid correctional facilities of amenities such as television and air conditioning. These demands have an intuitive appeal because no taxpayer wants to fund a comfortable lifestyle for prisoners. Yet the reality in prison is different from the one described by many of those who want to toughen conditions. Three out of four inmates in the United States are housed in overcrowded facilities where the living space for two people is the size of a walk-in closet. Some inmates suffer physical abuse in prison: In the high-security wing of an Oregon state prison, an inmate was stripped naked, placed in full mechanical restraints, and locked in a "quiet cell" with the lights on for twenty-four hours a day. He was not permitted out-of-cell exercise for five years. Others suffer sexual abuse: It has been estimated that almost one-quarter of all inmates are victims of a sexual assault each year during incarceration. Other prison systems are corrupt: Between 1989 and 1994, fifty correctional staff in the District of Columbia were convicted of serious crime, eighteen of them for smuggling drugs into prison for inmates. Many prisons are clean and well-administered, but no prison is luxurious. In some, life is so wretched that the courts have ordered authorities to improve conditions or face jail time themselves. For example, in 1994, thirty-nine states plus the District of Columbia were under court order to reduce overcrowding or improve prison conditions. It is partly because of these conditions that many offenders have such a difficult time making the transition to freedom.

Absurd Laws and Policies

The debate over prison conditions is often used to distract voters from the real problems facing the criminal justice system. In Mississippi, a law was passed banning individual air conditioners for inmates even though not a single inmate had an air conditioner. A Louisiana law forbids inmates from taking classes in karate or martial arts, even though there were no such training classes available. The governor of Connecticut blasted a prison for providing "country club" landscaping on the outside of the facility. In reality, the planting had been done at the request of nearby residents annoyed by the ugly prison wall. It appears that other new laws are intended to humiliate inmates. Mississippi began requiring inmates to wear striped prison suits with the word "convict" on the back. In Alabama, the governor reinstituted prison chain gangs. Inmates shackled together in groups of five "work" on state roadways chipping away at rocks, with no apparent purpose except to convince passersby something is being done about the crime problem.

For those concerned with public safety as well as vengeance, the issue of jail and prison conditions becomes more complicated. We all want inmates to feel the sting of punishment and loss of freedom. On the other hand, it does not serve public safety to so frustrate inmates that they return to the streets embittered and angry. Jail and prison conditions exert a significant influence on whether an inmate becomes productive upon release or resumes criminal behavior. More than nine out of ten inmates currently in prison will be released at some point. Although prisons cannot become "country clubs" without losing their deterrent effect, they also cannot become gulags without jeopardizing public safety. The best correctional facilities strike a balance between punishment and the opportunity for inmates to become self-sufficient, particularly as they get closer to release. . . .

EFFECTS ON THE FAMILY

Although we know that a stable family is one of the strongest bulwarks against a life of crime, so many men in our inner cities are incarcerated that it has become increasingly difficult there to create and sustain a two-parent family. For many young women in the inner city, there is a scarcity of available men of marriage age because so many are going in and out of jails and prisons. Moreover, about three out of four women in prison have children. Only 22 percent of these women say they can count on the fathers of their children to care for them while they are incarcerated. In some inner-city areas, virtually every resident has a close relative and over 50 percent have a parent who is in prison, on probation, on parole, in jail, or in hiding because there is a warrant out for their arrest.

THE FAILURE OF IMPRISONMENT

Nationally, every 7 minutes, another person enters prison. And every 14 minutes, someone returns to the streets, beaten down and, more often than not, having suffered a great amount of violence during his or her incarceration. Professionals will tell you that incarceration really does very little to stop crime, but we go on spending billions of dollars in order to lock up more and more people. We have become the country with the highest incarceration rate in the industrialized world.

Dave Kelly, *Salt of the Earth*, November/December 1995.

Many advocates of continued prison construction argue that longer sentences are necessary to protect families from crime. It is certainly appropriate to remove violent offenders from our streets. But the flip side of our crime policy is that the injudicious use of prison to incarcerate so many nonviolent offenders can undermine family structure by removing a large portion of the male population from community life. This reality must be weighed carefully by those who make criminal justice policy.

States all over the country are trimming and reorganizing their budgets, but taxpayers continue to pour money into prison construction and operations in a way that competes with funding for education and other quality-of-life programs. Five states have a corrections budget of over one billion dollars. California, which has the largest prison system of any state, spends $3.6 billion per year on prison operations and another $500 million per year on new prison construction. Nationwide, spending on corrections at the state level has increased faster than any other spending category. Preliminary data for fiscal year 1996 show average increases in appropriations for corrections over the previous year to be 13.3 percent, more than twice the increase for education. Prison has become a modern public works program: in Texas, the government spent more than $1 billion to add over 76,000 prison beds in two years and in 1995 planned to hire 12,000 employees to staff its new prisons. Spending on corrections at a national level has risen three times as fast as military spending over the last twenty years.

DIVERTED FUNDS

In order to fund jails and prisons, state and local governments have been forced to divert money from education and welfare spending. California is typical of the trend. Fifteen years ago, 3 percent of the state budget in California went to prisons while 18 percent was allocated for higher education. In 1994, the state spent 8 percent of its budget on prisons and 8 percent on higher education. Between 1994 and 1995 the overrun in corrections spending (an 11.1 percent actual increase compared to a 7.1 percent budgeted increase) was more than the entire increase in higher education (2.3 percent). From 1979 to 1990, state government expenditures nationwide rose 325 percent for prison operations and 612 percent for prison construction. Some states that have built prisons find they cannot afford to run them. In South Carolina, two prisons that cost $80 million recently stood empty because of a shortage of money. . . .

THE CASE OF THE DRUG DEALER

Imprisonment is a politically appealing response to fear because a person who is locked up obviously cannot commit a crime against a person on the outside. But the simplicity can be deceptive. Take the example of the typical small-time drug dealer. This offender has helped fuel the jail and prison expansion in recent years, yet it is also this offender who is most easily replaceable in the drug trade. Somebody else almost always steps in to take the place of the dealer when he or she goes to prison. Incarcerating the second drug dealer costs just as much as incarcerating the first. By the time the criminal justice system has passed through several generations of drug dealers, billions of dollars have been spent and the corner is still scattered with empty vials of crack cocaine.

"The power of imprisonment to prevent crime is unmatched by any other public policy strategy."

IMPRISONMENT REDUCES CRIME

Michael K. Block and Steven J. Twist

In the following viewpoint, Michael K. Block and Steven J. Twist contend that no policy is more effective at reducing crime than imprisonment. Block and Twist maintain that in the ten states with the highest increase in prison populations, crime rates declined more than 20 percent. At the same time, they argue, states that reduced their prison populations through early-release programs experienced a significant rise in crime. Block, a law and economics professor at the University of Arizona in Tucson, served on the United States Sentencing Commission from 1985 to 1989. Twist, assistant general counsel for Viad Corporation, served as Arizona's chief assistant attorney general from 1979 to 1991.

As you read, consider the following questions:

1. Why has the current criminal justice system become ineffective at deterring criminal conduct, in the authors' opinion?
2. According to Block and Twist, on which criminal justice policies do government leaders focus?
3. In the authors' opinion, what are the two most important measures needed to reduce crime?

Excerpted from Michael K. Block and Steven J. Twist, "Lessons from the Eighties: Incarceration Works," *Common Sense*, Spring 1994. Reprinted by permission of the authors.

A ccused serial killer Henry Louis Wallace, in Charlotte, North
Carolina, has experienced the collapse of America's criminal
justice system, and so have his alleged victims, now said to
number 11.

According to press accounts, in 1988 Wallace was convicted
of burglary in the state of Washington. His sentence was suspended, and he was given probation. He absconded from a probation violation, and a warrant was issued for his arrest. In
March 1990, he allegedly put a gun to the head of a 16-year-old
girl in South Carolina and attempted to rape her. He was arrested and released eight days later, when he was put into a
"pre-trial intervention" program, supposedly reserved for first-
time, nonviolent offenders.

In 1991, he was sent to prison for burglary convictions, but
was released after serving only four months. In February 1992,
despite the fact that he was a repeat offender with at least one
prior prison term, Wallace was freed on his own recognizance after being arrested for allegedly raping a 17-year-old girl, again at
gunpoint. He was later charged with the murder of 11 women.
Why didn't our system of justice from the beginning treat Wallace's crimes seriously and protect the innocent? From the beginning of Wallace's criminal career, the system failed, for whatever
reason, to serve the interests of those whom he is charged with
murdering.

Every day, on the streets of America, stories like this are repeated with frightening regularity. They are the cadence of violent crime, shattered lives, failed leniency, and fractured order.

VICTIMS OF VIOLENT CRIME

More than 6.5 million Americans will suffer the ordeal of crime
directly this year [1994], victims of murder, rape, robbery, or
aggravated assault. According to the Bureau of Justice Statistics,
five out of six 12-year-olds will be the victims of a violent
crime in their lifetimes. The collapse of America's criminal justice system is felt no more keenly than by the children who are
growing up in a world where fear of violent crime is their most
constant companion.

America was not always this violent; so what has changed?
The answers are, of course, complex. The straining of family
bonds and the weakened influence of those social and religious
institutions that have traditionally transmitted values in our
country surely are factors. And just as surely there are the seeds
of long-term solutions here. But America is in an immediate crisis of violent crime the dimensions of which we have not seen

in our lifetime, perhaps not in our history.

The most immediate threat we face is from a criminal justice system that is no longer effective at deterring criminal conduct because it has lost the will to punish. Every day in 1994, 14 people will be murdered, 48 women raped, and 578 people robbed by criminals who have already been caught, convicted, and then returned to the streets on probation or early parole. In 1994, more than 60,000 people will be convicted of a violent crime but not sent to prison, and of these, more than 10,000 will be repeat offenders. Indeed, in 1994 nearly 100,000 repeat offenders, including those with prior convictions for violent crimes, will be convicted of felonies and not sent to prison. For those convicted of a violent crime who are sent to prison, the average time served is only 3.8 years.

GETTING TOUGH WORKS

The crumbling of American order is now being accelerated by a unilateral retreat from the opening gains of the 1980s, when for the first time in decades skyrocketing crime rates turned around as imprisonment rates increased. But we are now on the verge of squandering the singular lesson of the 1980s regarding crime control: Getting Tough Works.

It is perhaps the best-kept secret in the country. We are constantly being told that America is now locking up more criminals than at any time in its history, and that these "record" imprisonment rates have had no effect on our crime rates. This "theory" now animates most of the policy initiatives on crime from the White House, the Justice Department, and the Congress. And yet, nothing could be further from the truth.

In 1960, 738 people were in prison for every 1,000 violent crimes. By 1980, the number had plunged to 227 as American criminal justice was in the grip of public policies that favored "rehabilitation" over punishment. Of course this collapse of punishment was accompanied by astonishing increases in crime. But in the 1980s, we started to climb out of this punishment trough as the notion was abandoned that society and not the criminal was the "root cause" of crime. By 1992, 423 people were in prison for every 1,000 violent crimes, clearly a dramatic turnaround but nowhere near approaching even the 1960 levels.

The crime control effects of this restoration of punishment were nothing less than dramatic. From 1980 to 1992, the 10 states that had the highest increase in their prison populations relative to total FBI index crime actually experienced, on average, a decline in their crime rates of more than 20 percent,

41

while the 10 states with the smallest increases in incarceration rates averaged almost a 9 percent increase in crime rates. Specifically in terms of violent crime, using the experience of all 50 states during this period, we estimate a 10 percent increase in the prison population per 1,000 violent crimes was associated with a 2 percent decline in the violent crime rate. [The FBI index is the number of crimes of murder, rape, robbery, aggravated assault, burglary, theft and motor vehicle theft, and arson reported per 100,000 population.]

THE CASE OF MICHIGAN

The lessons from individual states bear out the aggregate conclusions. In a 1992 study, the Justice Department found that in Michigan, funding for prison construction dried up in the early 1980s. The state instituted an early-release program and became one of only two states whose prison population declined from 1981 to 1984. Between 1981 and 1986, the rate of violent crime rose by 25 percent at the same time national crime rates were declining. In 1986, however, when Michigan embarked on a major prison building effort, the state's violent crime rate began to fall and by 1989 had dropped 12 percent.

MORE TIME REDUCES CRIME

The Federal Bureau of Investigation reported in May 1995 that the rate of violent and serious crimes had dropped 3 percent in 1994, the third consecutive year of decline. Some cities, including New York, have reported a significant decrease in homicide.

Representative Bill McCollum, the Florida Republican who is chairman of the House subcommittee on crime, called the report "encouraging" and said it showed that Congress's efforts to stop crime by lengthening prison sentences and building more prisons were beginning to work.

"If you can get these violent criminals to serve more time, you will inevitably reduce the violent crime rate," Mr. McCollum said. "Anyone who is locked up will not commit a crime."

Fox Butterfield, New York Times, August 10, 1995.

Indeed, there is overwhelming empirical evidence that punishing criminals reduces crime. According to Professor Donald Lewis, who surveyed the results of the 15 most rigorous empirical studies on the matter, increasing the length of imprisonment for FBI index crimes by 10 percent has been estimated to decrease the index crime rate by about 5 percent. For crimes against the person, it is estimated that a 10 percent increase in sentence length yields about a 2 percent decrease in the violent crime rate.

Using Professor Lewis' methodology, we reviewed the academic literature on estimates of deterrent effects and found that increases in the certainty of punishment (i.e., the likelihood of being imprisoned after conviction) have an even more powerful deterrent effect. Increasing the certainty of punishment for those convicted of a violent crime by 10 percent is estimated to reduce violent crime by about 7 percent.

The demonstration of the relative deterrent effects of increases in certainty and severity are even more enlightening when expressed in offense terms. By increasing the length of sentence served by violent offenders by 4.5 months, it is likely that 40,000 violent crimes could be averted each year. If the number of violent criminals sent to prison increases by as few as 9,000 each year, about 140,000 violent crimes could be prevented each year. In order to accomplish this, both strategies require about the same new prison bed space.

A COST-EFFECTIVE APPROACH

If the best-kept secret of the 1980s was that getting tough worked to begin to control crime, that it was also cost-effective comes in a close second. Professor Mark Cohen of Vanderbilt University has demonstrated that for violent crimes other than robbery, increasing the length of sentence by 10 percent has a cost-benefit ratio of about three—in other words, the victim losses averted are about three times greater than the cost incurred by increasing the length of imprisonment. For all violent crimes, increasing the certainty of punishment averts about twice as much in losses for victims as the cost of the additional prison capacity needed to increase imprisonment rates. For rape, the benefits of increasing the likelihood of imprisonment are six times greater than the costs of the policy change. These findings are confirmed by other research conducted by Professors John DiIulio and Anne Piehl. Their conclusions, published in *Brookings Review*, found "for every dollar society spent to keep a prisoner locked-up, it averted nearly two dollars in social costs—a wise social investment."

Unfortunately, the "policy wonks" in the White House, the Justice Department, and the Congress have different investments in mind. Their focus is on treatment, counseling, and therapy. But the 1980s have also given us some hard evidence on the failures of these approaches. For example, drug treatment programs have been found to have no significant impact on crime and little impact on drug abuse. Juvenile delinquency prevention, diversion, and treatment programs have shown few, if any, successes. Even attempts to use individual or group psychotherapy to reduce recidivism rates of delinquents and criminals show "little evidence" of a "beneficial effect," according to James Q. Wilson and Richard J. Hernstein.

The evidence is clear, and the lessons from the 1980s are irrefutable. We must build enough prison capacity to lock up every violent and repeat offender, and to keep them, at least the most serious violent offenders, locked up for substantially more time. . . .

PRISONS ARE THE KEY

Contrary to what we have been told by the anti-prison lobby in this country, prisons are the key to increasing the personal safety of the American people. The power of imprisonment to prevent crime is unmatched by any other public policy strategy. The two most important things that the federal government can do to reduce crime in America are to help the states build prison capacity, and stop the escalation of the costs of prison construction and operation.

When viewed in the context of our history, this agenda for prison building is a modest one. It builds on the clear vision of the American people who want swift and certain punishment. Those who fight against prisons in favor of more money for social programs to fight crime have it exactly backwards. Our first duty is to clear the streets of violent and repeat offenders and to restore integrity to our laws. This bold step will create the climate where in time other programs can flourish. Given the crisis of today, we must embark on an agenda now to build more prisons, operate them cheaply and efficiently, and enact tough sentencing laws in order to create conditions for order and freedom to prevail.

"Prisons . . . have not had a
significant effect on reducing overall
crime."

IMPRISONMENT DOES NOT REDUCE
CRIME

Campaign for an Effective Crime Policy

The nonpartisan Campaign for an Effective Crime Policy was
created in 1992 by a group of criminal justice officials in Washington, D.C. In the following viewpoint, the campaign argues
that misleading evidence has been used to support the theory
that imprisonment reduces crime. In actuality, the campaign asserts, studies show that incarceration does not result in a reduction of crime rates. The authors also maintain that increased incarceration has no deterrent effect on criminals.

As you read, consider the following questions:
1. What is the general deterrence theory, according to the
   campaign?
2. According to the campaign, what percentage of serious
   felonies are unreported or unsolved?
3. In the authors' opinion, what do arrest rates for robbery
   show?

Excerpted from the Campaign for an Effective Crime Policy's briefing paper "What Every
Policymaker Should Know About Imprisonment and the Crime Rate," February 1995, by
permission of the publisher.

The number of Americans in prison has quadrupled during the past twenty years. The reasons for this are complex and include deep concern about crime; the erosion of the rehabilitative ideal; increased emphasis upon punishment as an overriding goal of the criminal justice system; changes in sentencing practices, including the increasing use of mandatory minimum sentences; and the escalation of crime as a potent political issue.

While the actual interplay of these and other factors on the use of imprisonment may be debatable, three issues are not: 1) Prison plays an essential role in isolating dangerous offenders from the community; 2) The cost of prison to the taxpayers is very high; and 3) Taxpayers are promised that what they are buying for their money is less overall crime.

THE LIMITED IMPACT OF INCARCERATION

The cost of imprisonment is well documented and needs no further elaboration here. But what of the promise of less crime? Careful analysis of research in this area leads to the following conclusions:

- It is very difficult to measure the effect of incarceration on crime rates.
- Incarceration appears to have no significant effect upon violent crime rates.
- Incarceration appears to have a marginal effect on property crime rates.

The reasons that incarceration has a limited impact on crime include the following:

1. A wide variety of economic and social factors outside the control of the criminal justice system contribute to crime rates.
2. Demographics show that overall crime rates tend to rise and fall with the number of males in the crime-prone 15- to 24-year-old age group.
3. The criminal justice system deals with only a small fraction of crimes committed.
4. The criminal justice system is unable to accurately identify high risk offenders early in their criminal careers.
5. The threat of longer prison sentences does not deter violent crime, since most violent crime is committed impulsively, often under the influence of alcohol or drugs.
6. For some crimes, especially drug crimes, new recruits quickly take the place of those confined.

This viewpoint will examine these matters in greater detail.

The theory that increased incarceration reduces crime rates is based on two assumptions: that the *incapacitation* of offenders prevents those particular individuals from committing more crimes for the duration of their incarceration, and that the greater threat of imprisonment *deters* those released from prison and other potential criminals from acting on a criminal impulse. It is thought that if more criminals face incarceration for their crimes, society will gain a corresponding decrease in crime rates.

Incapacitation theory focuses on the fact that while an individual is in prison, he or she cannot commit more crimes. A related idea is that of *selective incapacitation*, the theory that society can predict who the most serious offenders will be in the future based on certain characteristics and past behavior. Some studies show that a small but active percentage of the criminal population commits a substantial portion of crime. Thus, it is asserted not only that incapacitating more offenders reduces crime, but that if the criminal justice system can learn to identify and imprison the high-risk group of offenders early in their criminal careers, the overall crime rate will decrease even more dramatically.

General deterrence is concerned with the effect of incarceration on persons other than the imprisoned offender. Deterrence theorists argue that a person who otherwise would choose to commit a crime is prevented from doing so by the perception of certainty or severity of punishment which may await.

PRISON REINFORCES CRIMINAL ATTITUDES

While the public tends to believe that prison will teach the offender a lesson and he will no longer commit crimes, in reality the opposite is more often the truth. Prison reinforces crime patterns and makes the offenders more likely to repeat crimes, especially violent ones.

The nationwide recidivism (or return) rate for prison inmates is 70 percent, and graduates of our prison system usually progress toward more serious crimes. This is because prison inmates must learn and adhere to an "inmate code" to survive. This code emphasizes racism, retaliatory violence and predatory attitudes regarding sex and property.

Robert W. Winslow, *San Diego Union-Tribune*, August 28, 1994.

It is difficult to test theories about the impact of imprisonment on crime rates. Just because two facts exist does not necessarily mean there is a cause and effect relationship between them. For example, few people would agree that if crime rates rose when the imprisonment rate rose that the increase in imprisonment *caused* the increase in crime. One immediately asks what else was going on that might influence these trends.

The relationship between imprisonment and crime is very difficult to ascertain, in part because it is difficult to isolate these factors from other social and economic variables which probably influence the level of crime, such as demographic shifts, unemployment rates, divorce rates, and education levels. Recent research on the relationship between increased incarceration and crime rates has attempted to correct for such external factors, with mixed results. Clearly, imprisonment has an incapacitative effect on the individual offender. The key issue, however, is whether increased imprisonment (for either incapacitative- or deterrence-based reasons) results in an overall decrease in crime, and at what cost.

The simplest way to begin examining the relationship of increased incarceration to crime is to look at actual crime and incarceration rates over time to see whether increased incarceration does lead to a decrease in the crime rate.

How Crime Rates Are Measured

National crime rates are measured by two basic methods: police reports and victimization surveys. Although each has different advantages to its methodology, neither is entirely satisfactory for the purpose of measuring changes in the crime rate. Weaknesses in both methods can lead to easy manipulation of crime statistics and misleading results.

The first method, the Uniform Crime Reports (UCR), is tabulated from police reports and thus is limited to crimes actually reported to the police. The advantage of the UCR is that it includes homicides in its calculation of the violent crime rate. The disadvantage to using the UCR is that much crime is never reported to the police and thus the UCR provides an incomplete representation of actual crime committed. In addition, trends in official statistics may be the result of changes in public reporting and police recording practices, not of actual changes in the amount of crime.

The second method, the National Crime Victimization Survey (NCVS), is the product of an annual random sampling of households conducted by the U.S. Census Bureau. Many scholars believe that the NCVS is a more reliable indicator of actual crime rates because the statistics are not dependent on victims' having reported the crimes to the police. However, being a victimization survey, the NCVS omits two important crimes, homicides and drug crimes. The latter is a significant omission, since a shift in criminal activity from an included crime (e.g., burglary, robbery) to drug dealing would appear as a decrease in the overall crime rate when no actual decrease had occurred.

National crime rates are divided into two general categories: violent crime and property (or non-violent) crime. Violent crime includes homicide, rape, robbery and assault. Property crime includes such offenses as burglary, larceny theft and auto theft. Distinguishing between the two, as this viewpoint does, provides a clearer picture of precisely which crimes are affected when "the crime rate" goes up or down, though these categories are themselves very broad and include very different behaviors within each.

MISLEADING EVIDENCE

1. *Time Frames Give Different Pictures.* Data on crime and incarceration rates is often used misleadingly in an attempt to demonstrate a correlation between the two statistics. It is common to see graphs and charts juxtaposing a declining crime rate with a rising incarceration rate, thereby "proving" that one directly affects the other. In fact, such charts are easily manipulated by choosing certain base years. During the course of each decade over the last thirty years, crime rates have experienced periods of sharp increase, slight decrease, and steady plateaus. Depending upon which base years are chosen, it is simple to manipulate short-term statistics to show almost any desired result. . . .

The Sentencing Project examined the claim that increased incarceration during the 1980s had slowed the rising UCR violent crime rate, and found the choice of time frame to be misleading. First, 1980–81 was an historically peak year for crime rates, and a dramatic increase from the years immediately before. Thus, the decade began with an anomalous record crime high. Had the time frame been, for instance, 1975–85, the overall change in the crime rate would have been much less marked. Second, the analysis found two distinct trends in the crime rate during the 1980s and early 1990s. From 1980 to 1986, incarceration rose by 65% while violent crime declined by 16%. From 1986 to 1991, incarceration rose by 51%, but violent crime actually *increased* by 15%. This increase in violent crime, occurring simultaneously with a large increase in incarceration, contradicts any claim of a direct relationship between violent crime and incarceration.

2. *Shifts in Victimization.* Another problem in looking at the relationship between crime and incarceration has to do with possible shifts in the types of victimization over time. The use of

NCVS data, which showed a 13% decrease in overall crime in the 1980s, illustrates this issue. The rate of burglaries and thefts did decline in the 1980s, leading some criminologists to suggest the existence of a link between property crime and incarceration rates. It is unclear, however, whether a causal relationship actually exists. The change may be due to other factors, such as a widespread shift from property crimes to other types of crime. For example, the amount of auto theft and drug trafficking—the latter a crime unreported by the NCVS—increased markedly during the same period despite higher incarceration rates for these offenses. As criminologist Joan Petersilia has noted, even the most cursory examination of today's inner cities would reveal a shift in street crime from the riskier crime of burglary to the more lucrative crime of drug dealing. Thus, a decline in the NCVS burglary rate does not necessarily mean that less crime is being committed; rather, it may indicate that offenders are opting to commit different crimes. This raises a serious question about the accuracy of the "decrease" in crime.

3. *Lack of a Substantial Correlation Between Crime and Incarceration.* It is undeniable that, over certain base years, the incarceration rate increased at the same time that the relative crime rate decreased. It is wrong to assume, however, that a direct causal relationship exists without exploring the many other factors, such as changes in demographics, unemployment rates, illegitimate birth rates, etc., which affect the crime rate. The evidence does not show a reliable correlation between violent crime and incarceration rates. At best, a slight correlation may exist between the incarceration rate and the property crime rate.

This issue was examined as well by the National Research Council in its study *Understanding and Preventing Violence*. To the question "What effect has increasing the prison population had on levels of violent crime," they responded, "Apparently, very little," concluding that "preventive strategies may be as important as criminal justice responses to violence.". . .

WHY DOESN'T INCARCERATION MORE SIGNIFICANTLY REDUCE CRIME?

A. *The criminal justice system only deals with a fraction of crimes committed and thus is limited in its ability to affect crime rates.* Approximately 90% of all serious felonies are never reported to the police, or go unsolved. Thus, 90% of serious crime is never handled by the criminal justice system. The effect of changes in crime policy is necessarily limited by the actual impact that the criminal justice system has on crime.

B.*We are not yet able to identify high-risk offenders early in their criminal careers.* Selective incapacitation—the process of earmarking potentially serious and repeat offenders and incarcerating only that percentage of the criminal population—has been discredited by most criminal justice experts for three reasons.

First, it is extremely difficult to identify high-risk offenders early in their criminal careers. Most studies which have attempted to do so result in an unacceptably high number of "false positives"—that is, they identify far more offenders as dangerous than is actually the case.

Second, incarcerating high-risk offenders in anticipation of future criminal behavior raises serious legal and ethical concerns. Serious offenders are disproportionately young males from identifiable racial and ethnic groups. However, the use of such factors in determining sentence length clearly would raise fundamental ethical and constitutional issues.

Third, choosing which offenders to earmark as "high-risk" can be an extremely politicized process. High-profile crimes, such as carjacking or stalking, often are the subject of disproportionate political attention. This attention easily results in pressure to classify the perpetrators of such crimes as "high-risk," when in fact they may not be, particularly in comparison to other crimes. In such a highly charged atmosphere, any attempts at selective incapacitation are easily sabotaged.

C.*We imprison criminals just as they are least likely to commit more crime.* Much violent crime is committed by the young. These offenders are either too young to go to prison, or are given lighter sentences for first-time felony convictions. Most jurisdictions concentrate on incapacitating habitual convicted offenders, who are identified only late in their careers when the amount of crime they commit is on the decline. Thus, states imprison many offenders at a time when they would commit relatively few crimes.

For example, arrest rates for robbery show that these offenders are at the peak of their criminal careers at the age of 18–19, and that rates of robbery by the age of 24 are half the peak rate. However, an offender convicted of robbery is twice as likely to go to prison at the age of 23 than at the age of 19.

No Deterrent Effect

D. *Increased incarceration fails to have a deterrent effect on violent crime.* Deterrence theory is premised on the assumption that each of us is a rational actor who will weigh all options and possible consequences before deciding whether to perform a particular act. If the risk of an undesired consequence outweighs the potential benefits, then we will choose not to act. Thus, proponents of increased incarceration argue that if society sufficiently increases the severity of an undesirable consequence (i.e. a prison sentence), potential criminals will choose not to break the law. This argument is unsupported by existing deterrence research. . . .

Furthermore, it is important to look closely at what deterrence studies reveal about the effect of harsher sentences on potential criminals. The imprisonment risk for committing a crime actually has two very separate components: the risk of apprehension (or certainty of punishment) and the risk of imprisonment once apprehended (or severity of punishment). While several exhaustive deterrence studies have cautiously concluded that there may be a slight deterrent effect if the risk of apprehension is increased, most deterrence researchers "doubt that increased penalties pay similar dividends," according to Franklin Zimring and James A. Hawkins. Thus, it appears that a potential criminal may be deterred if he believes that there is an increased risk of being caught by the police; however, where the risk of apprehension is constant, his behavior is not affected by a greater risk of being sent to prison for a longer period of time if caught.

The inconclusiveness of deterrence research cannot be overemphasized. After conducting an exhaustive study of deterrence, the prestigious National Academy of Sciences Panel on Research on Deterrent and Incapacitative Effects concluded that "policy makers in the criminal justice system are done a disservice if they are left with the impression that the empirical evidence, which they themselves are frequently unable to evaluate, strongly supports the deterrence hypothesis." With respect to increased incarceration in particular, existing research fails to demonstrate any deterrent effect of increased severity of punishment on crime rates. The act of committing a crime rarely is performed with sufficient forethought for the risk of a longer prison sentence to affect an offender's choice. . . .

Much political rhetoric has suggested a correlation between increased incarceration and reduced crime, when none or little actually exists. Prisons play the essential role of incapacitating dangerous felons, but have not had a significant effect on reducing overall crime. The factors which determine crime rates are more numerous, much more complex, and most are not within the control of the criminal justice system, through incarceration or other means.

PERIODICAL BIBLIOGRAPHY

The following articles have been selected to supplement the diverse views presented in this chapter. Addresses are provided for periodicals not indexed in the *Readers' Guide to Periodical Literature*, the *Alternative Press Index*, the *Social Sciences Index*, or the *Index to Legal Periodicals and Books*.

Teresa Albor — "The Women Get Chains," *Nation*, February 20, 1995.

John J. DiIulio Jr. — "Prisons Are a Bargain, by Any Measure," *New York Times*, January 16, 1996.

David R. Francis — "Just Proven: Prisons Do Keep Down Crime," *Christian Science Monitor*, January 19, 1996. Available from One Norway St., Boston, MA 02115.

Don M. Gottfredson — "Prison Is Not Enough," *Corrections Today*, August 1995.

Jesse Jackson — "Prisons Are One of Our Leading Growth Industries," *Liberal Opinion Week*, September 4, 1995. Available from PO Box 468, Vinton, IA 52349.

Anne Morrison Piehl and John J. DiIulio Jr. — "'Does Prison Pay?' Revisited: Returning to the Crime Scene," *Brookings Review*, Winter 1995.

Roger T. Pray — "How Did Our Prisons Get This Way?!" *Prison Mirror*, May 1, 1996. Available from PO Box 55, Stillwater, MN 55082-0055.

Vincent Schiraldi — "Some Gift—for $1.4 Billion, We Pay $31 Billion," *Los Angeles Times*, March 15, 1995. Available from Reprints, Times Mirror Square, Los Angeles, CA 90053.

Marilyn Berlin Snell and Bo Lozoff — "Habitat for Inhumanity," *Utne Reader*, September/October 1995.

Julie E. Tomz — "Prison Privatization in the U.S.," *Overcrowded Times*, April 1996. Available from PO Box 110, Castine, ME 04421-0110.

Robert W. Winslow — "Why Prisons Are Making Crime Worse," *San Diego Union-Tribune*, August 28, 1994. Available from 350 Camino de la Reina, San Diego, CA 92108-3003.

HOW SHOULD PRISONS TREAT INMATES?

Chapter Preface

Rehabilitation of prisoners has long been a goal of America's prison systems. In the 1970s, however, several researchers concluded that rehabilitation had largely failed as a strategy to reform inmates. These influential studies led to a change in corrections policies that deemphasized rehabilitation programs—education, job training, drug rehabilitation, and workshops aimed at controlling violent behavior—in favor of simple punishment. The sting of imprisonment, many officials theorized, would convince offenders to renounce criminal behavior.

Many experts today continue to argue that rehabilitation does not benefit inmates. They contend that the high recidivism rate among prisoners is proof that rehabilitation programs do not work. *U.S. News & World Report* senior editor Ted Gest agrees with this assessment; he writes, "One of the main reasons the revolving door keeps turning is that few criminals are rehabilitated in prison." According to clinical psychologist Stanton E. Samenow, the very idea of rehabilitation rests on a misconception. He argues, "To rehabilitate is to restore to a former constructive capacity or condition. *There is nothing to which to rehabilitate a criminal.* There is no earlier condition of being responsible to which to restore him."

However, proponents of rehabilitation argue that although these programs may not succeed with habitual or violent offenders, prisons should not therefore abandon rehabilitation attempts for all prisoners. Prisons should do more to help as many inmates as possible to become productive citizens, these commentators insist. In the words of Kenneth E. Hartman, imprisoned in California for murder, "Prison should be, and currently is not, a place where those who have earned separation from the free world are afforded the means to become whole." Although Hartman concedes that punishment is a necessary goal for prisons, he argues that rehabilitation is also essential. Other critics maintain that simply warehousing inmates without providing rehabilitative programs will never reduce crime or the prison population.

Observers continue to disagree about whether prisons should stress punishment or rehabilitation. This issue is among the topics debated in the following chapter on how prisons should treat their inmates.

| "The most desirable penal policy is that of just punishment, the swift punishing of blameworthy behavior."

PRISONS SHOULD PUNISH INMATES

Francis T. Murphy

Prisons were constructed as a humane alternative to public floggings and executions that were originally used to punish criminals. They were intended not merely to punish, but to rehabilitate convicts. Francis T. Murphy, the presiding justice of the New York Supreme Court Apellate Division First Judicial Department, argues in the following viewpoint that efforts to rehabilitate criminals have been ineffective. He concludes that the rehabilitative ideal should be abandoned and that criminals should be punished for breaking society's moral rules.

As you read, consider the following questions:

1. What factors does the author cite to support his assertion that the public no longer believes that criminal behavior can be changed?
2. Why, according to Murphy, should punishment be the goal of prison?
3. What standards must people hold themselves to, according to the author?

Francis T. Murphy, "Moral Accountability and the Rehabilitative Ideal," New York State Bar Journal, January 1984. Copyright 1984, New York State Bar Association. Reprinted with permission.

W hen a man is sentenced and led from courtroom to prison, two statements have been made as the door closes behind him. The judge has spoken to his crime, and society has spoken of how it will deal with him. Embedded in these statements is a fascinating complex of ideas about the nature of man, morality, law, and politics.

Prior to the 1800's, the prison system was unknown. Society's answer to the felon was usually given at the end of a rope or the swing of an axe. In imposing sentence, a judge was virtually a clerk, for he had no discretion in the matter. He simply sent the defendant to a death commanded by law.

During the first half of the 1800's, however, a confluence of ideas and political events produced the prison in America. So unusual was the idea of the prison that Europeans came to America in order to visit prisons and record what they saw.

THE IDEA OF PRISONS

How did the idea of the prison originate? In part, the prison was a humane answer to the criminal. Hanging a man for stealing a spoon or forging a note seemed immoral. In great part, the prison was an economic indulgence, for prior to the Industrial Revolution society could not have afforded prisons. Yet, lying behind humane motives and the new economy was a belief that included much more than the prison. The first half of the 1800's was an age of reform. Belief in the perfectibility of human beings and in the improvement of their social institutions was prevalent. In America and Europe a liberalism traceable to thinkers like John Locke and Desiderius Erasmus, to the Renaissance and ancient Greece, had as its central principle that to every question there was a rational answer, that man was able to discover rational solutions to his problems, and when thus enlightened he could live in a harmonious society. It was natural that a belief of that magnitude, infused into economic and social problems of every kind, and joined with a humanitarian spirit and the new, industrial wealth, would inhibit the tying of the rope and the swinging of the axe. Thus it was that the first half of the 1800's introduced in America not only the prison as a place for punishment and deterrence, but the prison as a place for the rehabilitative ideal, today condemned by many as the right idea in the wrong place.

THE REHABILITATIVE IDEAL

A usable definition of the rehabilitative ideal is that a primary purpose of penal treatment is the changing of the character and behavior of the prisoner in order to protect society and to help him. It is an idea that has attracted groups who march to the beat of very different drums. It has attracted those who think of crime as an individual's moral failure, or as an evil caused by corrupt social institutions, or as an entry in the printout of a prisoner's genetic program. Accordingly, the rehabilitative ideal has elicited different means—extending from the early 1800's imposition of absolute silence upon all prisoners in New York, and the unrelieved solitary confinement of all prisoners in Pennsylvania, to the twentieth century's faith in therapeutic interventions, such as the promoting of literacy, the teaching of vocational skills, the use of psychotherapy, and the less popular surgical removal of brain tissue. All of these means have one thing in common. Each has failed as a reliable rehabilitative technique and each, ironically, has today drawn public anger not upon those working in the rehabilitative disciplines, but upon very visible judges few of whom, if any, purport to be competent in any rehabilitative skill. Indeed, it is an anger that has a sharp edge, for though judges observe a traditional silence when accused of failing to rehabilitate the imprisoned, judges nevertheless have legislatively or constitutionally been drawn within the range of public attack in other areas of the rehabilitative ideal—sentencing discretion, the indeterminate sentence, probation, parole, and prison conditions.

PROPER PUNISHMENTS

To have any deterrent effect, punishments must be as immediate as possible, short-run in impact, and harsh in effect. Distant, long-run, relatively mild punishments have zero deterrent effect and possibly, where prisoners have room, board, and cable TV provided free of charge, even negative effect.

Richard T. Gill, *Public Interest*, Fall 1994.

Notwithstanding that the rehabilitative ideal never actually dominated the criminal justice system as a value prior to punishment and deterrence, it was generally believed by the public and the Bench that it had that primacy. In any case, substantial defections from that ideal began in the 1960's, not only among editorial writers and politicians but among scholars as well. Today, the ideal is incanted solemnly at sentence, but even then neither Bench nor counsel discuss it.

Why has the rehabilitative ideal depreciated so sharply? The answer must be traceable to ideas that drain belief in the notion of the mutability of human character and behavior. I will point to several of them.

PERVASIVE PESSIMISM

The nineteenth century belief in the simplicity and perfectibility of human nature has been profoundly shaken by the Freudian [Austrian psychoanalyst Sigmund Freud] revolution, to say nothing of the unprecedented savagery of the twentieth century. There is in America a continuing and almost apocalyptic increase in crime, notwithstanding that our average sentence is the longest in the Western world. Inevitably, a sense of helplessness, a foreboding of a collapse of public order is present at every dinner table. As for confidence in the utility of traditional therapeutic means, it has all but vanished. Indeed, it is generally accepted that a rehabilitative technique of any kind is yet to be discovered. Belief in the power of the public educational system to perform its simplest objective has been lost, hence the claims of education are not received as once they were. There has been a profound depression in the structure and authority of the family, and with it a decline of those family virtues associated with rehabilitation. A pervasive pessimism, an almost open contempt, for government has seeped into the public mind. A new mentality has arisen, markedly anti-intellectual in orientation, disclosing in American culture a sense of dependency, a seeking out of comfort and self-awareness, a flight from pain and personal responsibility. Moral passion has not declined. It has disappeared. These social facts are fragments of deeper changes which strikingly distinguish the major political movements of the twentieth century from those of the nineteenth. As Isaiah Berlin has observed, two devastating elements, traceable to Freud or Karl Marx, have united in the political movements of the twentieth century. One is the idea of unconscious and irrational influences that outweigh reason in explaining human conduct. The other is the idea that answers to problems exist not in rational solutions but in the extinguishing of the problems by means other than thought. So it is that the rehabilitative ideal, congenial to the essentially intellectual age of reform of the early 1800's, has depreciated with the twentieth century's devaluation of the intellect and the will. Looking back over the past two centuries, we see that science, as a new way of knowing, not only promised to augment man's power but dramatically delivered on that promise. The power it delivered, however, proved to be over nature only. It did not increase our power over ourselves to become better people. It has left man unchanged, sitting, as it were, in the evening of his life in a warehouse filled with his technology.

PRISONS ARE FOR PUNISHMENT

We are thus living at a critical point in the shaping of an American penal policy. We could increase penal sanctions by matching brutality for brutality, but ethics and utility argue against it. In any case, a political consensus fortunately does not support what is essentially a regressive, primitive gesture. Equally without a political consensus are programs for social reforms directed at what some think to be causes of crime—unemployment, racial discrimination, poor housing. Whether such conditions cause crime is disputed and, in any case, a penal policy is too narrow a platform upon which a plan of social reform can be based.

In my opinion, the most desirable penal policy is that of just punishment, the swift punishing of blameworthy behavior to the degree of the offender's culpability. By such a policy we reaffirm the reality of moral values. Thus we answer those who challenge the conception of man's moral responsibility. Thus we create hope in a future based upon ancient moral truths from which so many have drifted into a night of philosophical neutrality.

PRISONS, REHABILITATION DON'T MIX

The idea of just punishment has a wide consensus. It is a statement of a natural, moral intuition. It declares the moral autonomy of man without which all value systems are bound to be anarchic. It recaptures the lost community of moral and legal elements which once characterized crime and punishment, and without which a society loses its stability. As for the rehabilitative ideal, it should be stripped of its pretentiousness, if not of its very name. It is a hope of changing behavior, and nothing more. It is a goal, not a reality. In prison it should be directed at objectives that can be realized, particularly the avoidance of the deformative influences of prison life. Efforts at rehabilitation might well be concentrated at the offender outside of the prison setting, the one place where rehabilitation might have a fair chance of accomplishment. Surely rehabilitation is unlikely in prisons in which minimum standards of personal safety, health, and humane treatment are often violated. Indeed one cannot leave the literature of penology without the conviction that, if he were required to design a place in which the behavior of a man could never be improved, he would draw the walled, maximum security prison, very much like those into which men were led for rehabilitation in the early 1800's and are kept until this very day.

This time in which we live need not be an age of cynicism and despair. There is no principle that compels us to accept the philosophical debris of history. This time can, if we would but will it, be an age in which the fixed human values of Western civilization are brought back into their natural ascendancy. They who believe that man is not truly free, and hence not truly responsible, who market man as a rational animal without free will, who recognize neither good nor evil but only what is personally useful or harmful, who find the rule of right and wrong only in the current opinion of men, all these are strangers in the West. The values of Western civilization are ultimately the standards of men who hold themselves accountable for their moral acts. Upon that accountability all social institutions rise and fall.

> "Rehabilitation has historically been an important motive underlying reform efforts that increased the humanity of the correctional system."

PRISONS SHOULD REHABILITATE INMATES

Louis B. Cei

Louis B. Cei is chairman of the Virginia Department of Corrections Central Classification Board in Richmond. In the following viewpoint, Cei asserts that although many experts oppose rehabilitation as a criminal justice philosophy, some prisoners can benefit from rehabilitation programs. Citing research that finds that many rehabilitation programs have successfully reduced recidivism among inmates, Cei concludes that corrections officials should focus on inmates and programs that yield the most benefits.

As you read, consider the following questions:

1. What types of programs did "planned intervention" encompass, according to Cei?
2. According to Ted Palmer, cited by the author, what is the proper question to ask regarding correctional programs?
3. In Cei's opinion, which rehabilitation programs are most effective?

Louis B. Cei, "The Prison Rehabilitation Debate in the 1990s." This paper was written in September 1996 expressly for inclusion in the present volume.

With the unprecedented increase in prisoners since the mid-1980s, it is appropriate to ask what is being done to prevent inmates from committing future murders, robberies and drug use. Over the last twenty years, rehabilitating prisoners has come under attack as a strategy to reduce recidivism. Academics, researchers and prison policy makers have concluded that rehabilitation is not effective in reducing crime rates.

Instead society has turned to incapacitation. Many states, including Virginia, have abolished parole and instituted fixed sentences. While these efforts have reduced the crime rate, they have not stemmed the tide of prison commitments. From 1993 to 1995, the crime rate dropped 3 percent nationally. However in those same years, prisoner populations increased from 855,000 to over 1 million.

Since America's prisons are going to have more inmates for longer periods of time, it is prudent to ask what can be done to reduce the chances of ex-cons robbing your home or carjacking your auto after their release from prison. What do the latest research reports reveal about prison program effectiveness in dealing with crime and recidivism?

THE REHABILITATION CONCEPT

Until 1974, rehabilitation was viewed as the cornerstone of crime control and correctional management. The rehabilitation concept was that to correct criminal behavior and gain release on parole, the inmate had to show progress in a program. Criminal activity eventually stops. But the concept supporting rehabilitation was to make the criminal stop sooner through planned intervention. This took the form of academic and vocational programs, group and individual counseling, and release programs such as probation, parole and work release.

However, by the late 1970s rehabilitation was dead. Mainly due to the writings of sociologist Robert Martinson, prison rehabilitation programs were viewed as ineffective. In Martinson's article "What Works—Questions and Answers about Prison Reform" (1974) and his book *The Effectiveness of Correctional Treatment* (1975), he concluded that "nothing works" in the way of rehabilitative programs changing offender behavior.

Martinson reviewed 231 treatment programs from 1945 through 1967 and stated, "With few and isolated exceptions, the rehabilitation efforts that have been reported so far have had no appreciable effect on recidivism."

During the 1980s and throughout the 1990s, conservatives and liberals alike used Martinson's findings to support their own conclusions about correctional policies. Conservatives blamed rehabilitation for rising crime rates, and renewed the concepts of retribution, deterrence and incapacitation. On the other hand, liberals attacked existing rehabilitative programs for their coercive nature and due process problems associated with parole release based on program participation, which is not afforded to every inmate. Accordingly, liberals concluded that prison commitments should be avoided altogether and replaced by probation or other community-based alternatives.

In short, rehabilitative programs seemed to cost too much, yield too little and threaten civil liberties.

TED PALMER'S RESEARCH

However, some researchers have attacked the anti-rehabilitation consensus. California Youth Authority researcher Ted Palmer has been a force to be reckoned with in his publications. In his 1975 article "Martinson Revisited," in the *Journal of Research in Crime and Delinquency*, Palmer closely examined Martinson's data and noted that 39 or 48 percent of the total programs evaluated were positive or partly positive. Palmer wrote, "For example, if out of ten studies of group counseling, three or four were associated with negative outcomes, then the findings for group counseling as a whole would be considered conflicting or contradictory, even though all remaining studies may have produced clear positive results."

Palmer elaborated on this theme in his 1978 book *Correctional Intervention and Research* and concluded that many correctional programs do work for many offenders. He noted, "Rather than ask 'What works' for offenders as a whole, we must increasingly ask which methods work best for which types of offenders and in which type of settings."

In the following 15 years, Palmer painstakingly examined hundreds of programs and published his findings in his 1992 book *The Re-emergence of Correctional Intervention*. First, the author notes that he believes that society still has a responsibility for making at least some assistance available to offenders as human beings. In addition, from a theoretical point of view intervention provides practical assistance, such as vocational or academic training, or psychological counseling, which punishment and incapacitation were not designed to do. The question is which assistance is effective.

Palmer concludes that 20 percent of all reasonably evaluated experimental treatment programs do in fact work. Based on the collective results from several hundred studies, experimental success rates exceeded those of control groups by 10 percent. He claims that only 10 percent of all experimental programs achieved worse results than controls.

Moreover, researchers Francis T. Cullen and Paul Gendreau also independently reviewed the rehabilitation debate in their article "The Effectiveness of Correctional Rehabilitation" in the *American Prison* (1989). They concluded that, based on 200 studies between 1973 and 1987, many programs showed reduction in recidivism from 10 to 30 percent. . . . Successful programs were found in family therapy, early intervention, probation, diversion and substance abuse.

Based on a review of all current studies, the most effective programs were the life skills and multi-modal programs.

The life skills program consists of academic and vocational training, outdoor experience and drug programs and in some cases interpersonal social skills training. Palmer asserts that "these growth centered approaches had gained strength in terms of focus, direction and perceived legitimacy."

A PLEA FOR HELP

On the tier where I live, here at the [Tehachapi, California] prison, a young gang member came to me a while back and asked for help in writing a plea to the prison administration. His words were simple and uneducated, but they had an eloquent power: "Please give me some education, or a trade, because I don't want to come back to prison."

In a rational system, this young man would have been afforded the opportunity to learn or develop a skill, but in the get-tough world of California prisons, he was not. What gave his words even greater urgency was the fact he will soon be paroled back to society, just as over 95 percent of us will, eventually.

Kenneth E. Hartman, *San Diego Union-Tribune*, July 2, 1995.

Likewise, multi-modal programs such as work-study, counseling and restitution were also most effective. Palmer writes "that certain combination of elements may have considerably more relevance to clients and in that sense, more power than any of those elements alone."

Despite all the theoretical and research attacks, rehabilitation remains the dominant aim of American criminal justice policy. As writers Francis Cullen and Karen Gilbert write in their book *Reaffirming Rehabilitation* (1982), "Rehabilitation is the only justification of criminal sanctioning that obligates the state to care for an offender's needs or welfare. . . . Rehabilitation has historically been an important motive underlying reform efforts that increased the humanity of the correctional system."

Every rehabilitative program does not work, and every prisoner cannot be rehabilitated. But some programs are effective for some prisoners. Correctional administrators at all levels need to focus on those inmates and those programs which will yield the highest benefits.

> "One way of controlling violence within a prison is to minimize the physical contact inmates have with one another."

VIOLENT OFFENDERS SHOULD BE PLACED IN MAXIMUM SECURITY

California Department of Corrections

California's Pelican Bay State Prison Security Housing Unit (SHU), located near the Oregon border, is the state's most secure prison facility. In the following viewpoint, the California Department of Corrections argues that the SHU is necessary in order to segregate the prison system's most violent offenders from other inmates and staff. The department maintains that high levels of security and supervision in the SHU ensure safety and cooperation.

As you read, consider the following questions:

1. How long do SHU terms last, according to the department?
2. According to the department, how are inmates escorted outside their pods?
3. How are inmate visits conducted, according to the author?

Text from "Pelican Bay State Prison Security Housing Unit," a flyer published in April 1996 by the California Department of Corrections. Used with permission.

California's most secure prison facility—the high-tech Security Housing Unit (SHU)—is located within the maximum custody Pelican Bay State Prison. Its purpose: to protect staff and male inmates throughout the system from the few most violent, predatory offenders.

The prison is geographically isolated, lying just south of the Oregon border near the coastal community of Crescent City, California. One side of the prison houses maximum custody inmates in general population—those who can hold jobs, go to school, and mingle with other inmates.

Those assigned to Pelican Bay's SHU (pronounced shoo) have none of these privileges. They have proven by their behavior in prison that they cannot be housed safely with general population inmates.

The 1,056-bed facility at Pelican Bay is one of two Security Housing Units the department currently operates. The other, a 512-bed facility at Corcoran State Prison, houses both SHU and protective custody inmates.

Not every inmate is "eligible" for SHU. Most are sent there for committing violent acts while in prison such as murder, assault, initiating a riot, threatening staff or other inmates, or being caught with a weapon. An administrative review committee considers the evidence and listens to the inmate and witnesses. If the charges are verified, inmates can be given a SHU term ranging from a few months to five years.

Known gang members and affiliates—especially those responsible for violence or intimidation within the prison—also can be assigned to SHU. Because there is no set term for gang members assigned to SHU, the department conducts a thorough investigation to document the inmate's gang activities and reviews his status every 120 days.

DESIGNED FOR MAXIMUM PROTECTION

Pelican Bay's SHU often is referred to as a "super-max" prison. It was designed to ensure the maximum protection for inmates and staff.

Most inmates are in single cells. Heavy, perforated cell doors limit an inmate's ability to assault others, without obstructing visibility into or out of a cell. Bunks are molded into the wall and toilets have no removable parts that could be used to make weapons. All clothing, bedding and personal effects are x-rayed before being placed in a cell. There are eight individual cells in each pod. A shower is located on each floor. Several overhead skylights flood each pod with natural light. Each pod has its own 26' by 10' exercise yard.

The pods are arranged in a semi-circle, like spokes of a wheel, with a centralized control room as the hub. The control room officer has a clear view of all six pods, also called cell blocks. The officer operates each door, controls the entrances and exits to each pod, and monitors movement in the exercise yards via closed circuit television.

The SHU complex encompasses both housing and support functions within a single building envelope. A secure system of corridors is monitored by control rooms. To aid in the secure operation of the complex, the upper level corridors are restricted to staff only. Heavy mesh grating on the floor of the upper corridor allows close scrutiny of activity below.

CONTROLLING MOVEMENT AND CONTACT

Most SHU inmates are allowed a limited amount of unescorted movement within the pod. For example, an inmate can walk alone from his cell to the shower or to the exercise yard. This reduces the frequency of physical contact between staff and inmates and greatly diminishes the risk of assault. Only one inmate at a time is allowed to move within the pod.

Before an inmate moves outside his pod, he is placed in restraints. He is escorted to secure areas within the SHU complex by two correctional officers. He may:

- Receive health services
- Meet with counseling or administrative staff
- Conduct legal research
- Attend classification, parole or disciplinary hearings
- Visit with family or friends (non-contact visits only)

One way of controlling violence within a prison is to minimize the physical contact inmates have with one another. Unlike other institutions where lower custody inmates provide support services, at Pelican Bay's SHU only staff have physical contact with inmates.

Staff in the housing unit deliver food trays, mail, canteen supplies, or medications. In the law library they process requests for information, transmit approved material between inmates, and deliver reference books. Those few SHU inmates who share a cell can exercise together. Otherwise, the inmates are kept separate from one another throughout the prison.

Inmates from the Level IV side of the institution do come into the building to prepare meals, operate the canteen, or assist with routine maintenance. These general population inmates are searched when they come and go, are closely supervised while inside, and are kept separate from those housed there. They also wear special jump suits to distinguish them from SHU inmates.

By enforcing this kind of separation, the prison eliminates the possibility that inmates can be used as go-betweens for information or contraband. Further, it ensures that no inmate has a position of greater status or access within the SHU.

HEALTH CARE

Each SHU facility offers a full range of health care services including emergency care, routine medical diagnosis and treatment, mental health consultation, and dental care.

In many instances, physicians can diagnose and treat inmates during their "rounds" to the housing units. Most medications are dispensed on site by medical technicians.

FOR IMPROVED SECURITY

By removing [supermaximum security] prisoners from the general inmate population, we can better protect correctional officers and cooperative inmates and reduce the lockdowns and other control measures that interfere with drug treatment, educational, vocational and prison industries programs.

Illinois governor Jim Edgar, press release, October 18, 1993.

Any inmate needing complex medical treatment, dental care or in-depth psychological counseling is escorted in restraints to the infirmary. If the problem is beyond the scope of the prison infirmary, the inmate will be transported to a community hospital for treatment. The prison provides round-the-clock security for any inmates removed from the institution.

LEGAL RESEARCH

SHU inmates are allowed reasonable access to the prison law library for research. Run by an accredited librarian, Pelican Bay's library maintains up-to-date legal texts and research materials.

Inmates schedule library time in advance. Small groups are escorted to the library then locked into individual cells for study. The court has ruled that inmates may share legal materials with each other. Security staff search the material for contraband or unauthorized messages before they make the transfer.

The law library is designed to allow inmates time for quiet study. However, a court decision also allows conversation between inmates in library cells.

Leisure Time

Because of the high security level of the SHU, all leisure time activities are strictly controlled.

Visiting—Family members and friends can visit SHU inmates on regularly scheduled visiting days. All visits are non-contact visits. The inmate is escorted into a small, secure cell. The visitor sits on the opposite side of a Plexiglas divider and communicates with the inmate via telephone.

Exercise—Inmates have access to the exercise yard at least 10 hours per week. For security reasons, no exercise equipment is allowed. The concrete exercise area measures 10' wide by 26' long by 18' high. One half of the top is covered with Plexiglas for protection during inclement weather. The other half is open to the air but covered with a heavy mesh screen. Video cameras mounted at either end of the yard allow constant surveillance of the inmate's movements by the control room officer inside.

Religion—Religious services and programs are offered to SHU inmates on an individual basis. Chaplains meet with inmates in the housing unit or at the cell door.

Entertainment—Inmates may have radios and television sets inside their cells. They must use earphones to listen to the programs.

| "To describe the environment at Pelican Bay in a nutshell, it is restrictive, repressive and demeaning."

OFFENDERS SHOULD NOT BE PLACED IN MAXIMUM SECURITY

C. Askari Kweli

C. Askari Kweli is a maximum-security inmate in California's Pelican Bay State Prison Security Housing Unit (SHU). In the following viewpoint, Kweli contends that he and other SHU inmates have suffered unnecessary physical and psychological abuse. Because it imposes isolation and refuses to offer education and work opportunities, according to Kweli, the facility breeds inmates' rage and animosity, which the public will have to deal with upon their release. Kweli concludes that inmates should not be isolated in maximum security units.

As you read, consider the following questions:

1. According to Kweli, what must he do to be released from maximum security?
2. How many hours of the day are SHU inmates confined to their cells, according to Kweli?
3. What does the author give as the reasons for inmates' incarceration in maximum security?

C. Askari Kweli, "Letter from Pelican Bay," Third Force, January/February 1995. Reprinted by permission of the Center for Third World Organizing.

I am currently confined in the infamous Security Housing Unit (SHU) at Pelican Bay State Prison. I am doing an indefinite term based solely on my alleged association with (not membership in) a prison gang. In the year 1985 confidential documentation was submitted to prison officials by unknown informants making false and fabricated statements against me. At that time, the information was not deemed important enough to use against me, yet in 1992, without any disciplinary infraction or other justification, it was decided by prison officials that this same unconfirmed documentation was enough to subject me to indeterminate confinement in the SHU until my expected release date in the year 2010.

The only way I can be released to a general prison is for me to "debrief" and become an informant of the state, which is not an option I would even consider.

CLASSIFIED AS "THREATS"

My indeterminate SHU confinement is not based on any recent disciplinary violations or behavioral problems other than my staunch refusal to cooperate with prison officials in their insidious policy and criteria for debriefing. I have not had a serious disciplinary infraction since 1988, yet I continue to be considered "a threat to the safety and security of the institution" by prison officials. This vindictive and incorrect classification has deprived me of all physical contact with both family and friends, and has subjected me to extreme conditions of sensory privation and psychological abuse.

It must be recognized and understood that a large percentage of the prisoners isolated and confined in Pelican Bay Prison's SHU are there for nondisciplinary reasons and are serving indeterminate SHU terms based solely on the fact that prison officials have found and are vigorously using a loophole in the due process requirements that allows them to classify select prisoners as "threats to the safety and security of the institution" without any worries about objections from the courts or society at large.

We are prohibited from participation in any credit-earning programs, neither work, nor education or even vocational training. Thus, most of us are left in suspended animation with virtually nothing to occupy our time and minds but the realization and continued contemplation of multiple forms of abuse that each of us has individually suffered and collectively been subjected to. This kind of environment is fertile ground for the growth of animosity and revenge.

Many of us are not even eligible for parole, despite over 20 years in confinement, not because of disciplinary or behavioral problems but rather solely because, as a matter of policy, parole is not granted by the Parole Board to anyone confined in the SHU.

RESTRICTIVE AND REPRESSIVE

To describe the environment at Pelican Bay in a nutshell, it is restrictive, repressive and demeaning. A few of the deprivations and treatment that we are subjected to on a daily basis are: strip searches anytime you leave your assigned cell; handcuffing and shackling anywhere you go, escorted by two guards; no physical contact with anyone (verbal communication is restricted to the 8 to 10 persons within your immediate area); only 90 minutes per day allowed for exercise outside your cell (the other 22 and a half hours are spent in your sensory deprivation cage) in an enclosed "dog walk"; no educational opportunities; restricted personal property allowed; and a maximum two-hour noncontact visit allowed per week for those fortunate enough to receive visits.

As prisoners, besides the conditions in the SHU our main complaints are: a lack of due process from a panel of unbiased committee members during disciplinary and classification hearings; inadequate medical treatment and the lack of adequate psychiatric evaluation and treatment; the constant and officially tolerated use of excessive force and verbal and psychological abuse by prison guards, directed for the most part against prisoners who dare to complain or refuse to accept inhumane treatment (this is done to instill fear and submissiveness in the prison population); the lack of an independent agency with the necessary authority to adequately investigate such excessive use of force claims against prison officials; inconsistent and inadequate access to the prison's law library; the refusal to allow SHU prisoners to help each other with pro se litigation; tampering, delay and destruction of personal mail. This list should give you some idea of the type of environment we are subjected to 24 hours a day, 7 days a week, for years at a time.

Most of my days and nights are spent reading, writing and contemplating past mistakes and how best to minimize the chances of those same mistakes recurring in my life. In dealing with the past and planning for the future, it is oftentimes hard to be optimistic when you don't really have anything to look forward to other than returning to the exact lifestyle that was a major contributing factor to landing in prison in the first place.

With all the emotion of the "get tough on criminals" attitude now running out of control, most members of society are able to delude themselves into forgetting that most of those in prison are destined for eventual release and we will have to be directly dealt with by society in one form or another. The physical and psychological abuse suffered, the rage and animosity harbored, and the revenge plotted will all rebound. Americans are condoning the creation of a being within these camps that they have never before seen the likes of, and unless they quit acting on emotion and begin to actually strive to resolve the many contradictions that exist in prison and in society this being will one day surface to haunt them and there will be no escape.

A Volatile Effect

Although there's no sure way to link later crimes with an inmate's prison experience, a growing number of psychiatrists and corrections experts say that intense and lengthy periods of isolation of prisoners can prove volatile for inmates already on the edge. Someday, they say, these men and women must return to the streets—and communities will have to cope with the results.

Sasha Abramsky and Andrew White, City Limits, June/July 1996.

The issue comes to the fore as to what type of prisoner does society wish to encounter and deal with upon their eventual parole? The options are: 1) a prisoner who has been subjected to an assortment of sadistic physical and psychological abuses sanctioned by society's desire to "get tough"; or 2) a prisoner who at least knows that he or she has been given a meaningful opportunity to rectify past mistakes and is encouraged to improve one's self and make a positive change in order to re-enter society and become a productive citizen. The choice is yours to make and act upon.

It must be realized that most of us are incarcerated in the SHU for reasons that have to do with economics. We are mostly from poor backgrounds, we don't have much education and we don't have the skills we need to make it in the job market. If we inside the SHU were given an opportunity to learn a viable trade most of us would take full advantage of it. Instead, the present politics of prison life coupled with the ulterior self-serving motives of politicians and prison officials makes this impossible. So what is to become of those of us who seek positive change but are being denied any constructive opportunity to bring this about?

An Issue for All

With about a million and a half men and women in prisons and jails in this country, these questions become larger and more important every day. Prison reform is not an issue only for prisoners; it should be a concern for all citizens who care about living in a just and safe society. A few essentials that should be demanded for prison reform are:

1. Mandatory educational and job training programs for all prisoners;

2. Community resources (in and out of prison) to enable the prisoner to stay in contact with the community and give the prisoner the chance to understand how his or her destructive acts have hurt the community. The goal should be to allow the prisoner to spend his or her time behind bars figuring out how best to utilize this time to rectify the past destructive acts and make the transition to being a constructive member of society;

3. Independent investigation and monitoring of prison officials' conduct;

4. Mechanisms of accountability so that prison officials cannot hide behind their claim of "qualified immunity" for acts of brutality;

5. Prison lobby and support groups, so that prisoners have a place to turn for help.

These reforms would at least give prisoners a way to have a positive impact on the institution. Citizens must stop allowing themselves to be duped into believing that those classified as the "criminal element" are the cause of all of society's ills, and begin to deal with the real causes of unemployment, homelessness, etc. Only then will we be able to create a society that is safe and beneficial for all its citizens, and not just the select few.

In conclusion, let me state that I am tired of words being sent to the outside world as an exercise in futility. I want them to be acted on until constructive change is brought about.

| "In most prisons, felons have access to a startling array of creature comforts."

PRISONS SHOULD NOT CODDLE INMATES

Robert James Bidinotto

Prisons are often criticized for providing entertainment, exercise equipment, and other amenities to inmates. In the following viewpoint, Robert James Bidinotto argues that inmates are coddled so much that America's prisons have become virtual resorts. Bidinotto contends that prisons throughout the United States have lost their emphasis on discipline and punishment and have increasingly allowed prisoners to live comfortably. Bidinotto writes on criminal justice issues for *Reader's Digest*, a monthly general interest magazine.

As you read, consider the following questions:

1. How much did prison weight lifters' injuries cost Arizona, according to Bidinotto?
2. According to John J. DiIulio, cited by the author, what group of people have become top prison officials?
3. What federal law have prisoners exploited, according to Bidinotto?

Mercer Regional Correctional Facility is a complex of tidy brick buildings situated in the rolling countryside of western Pennsylvania. From a distance, a visitor might mistake this state prison with its manicured green lawns for one of the nearby liberal-arts colleges.

In his office, Superintendent Gilbert Walters explains that Mercer's 850 convicted felons "aren't evil, by and large. Many just did not have good life circumstances and have reacted inappropriately." Walters, who began his career in counseling and refers to the inmates as "clients," tries to make the prison experience "as much like the street as I can."

It's hard to imagine that, for most of Mercer's "clients," life outside could be this good. One of the three full-time "activities directors" shows me the Recreation Building. "Nothing cheap here," he says proudly, pointing out the full-sized basketball court, handball area, punching bag and volleyball net. There are enough barbells to "bulk up" 15 criminals at a time; others can use weight-lifting machines. Nine electronic exercise bicycles and four stair-type aerobics machines face a TV, all part of the Leisure Fitness Program. Outside, the men can play softball and sharpen their tennis skills. Emotional problems? Five psychologists and ten counselors are there for Mercer's "clients."

Housing about a third of the inmates are two dormitories with eight-by-ten-foot "rooms" (not cells) equipped with desks and bookshelves. As we enter one room, a chubby, middle-aged man turns down the volume on his TV set. This housing unit, the guide says, shelters a "peer group" with "special needs": largely rapists and child molesters.

Mercer is not an exceptional institution; it is, in fact, typical. A nationwide *Reader's Digest* survey shows that in most prisons, felons have access to a startling array of creature comforts.

• Hard labor is out, physical fitness is in. From aerobics to strength training to boxing, today's thugs and armed robbers can return to the streets bigger, stronger and faster than ever.

• When they're tired of working out, they can join theater groups, take music lessons or college courses—all for free. Or they can tune in the latest R-rated movies.

• The overall cost of these prison amenities is soaring. They take up a huge portion of state correctional budgets, while thousands of violent criminals are released each year for lack of space.

Inside New York's maximum-security Attica prison, which houses many of the Empire State's most violent felons, there is an incongruous sight: three small white buildings, which some staffers call "the hotel." Here, a counselor schedules up to 18 inmates per week for sex with their wives. New York offers such facilities for so-called private family visits at 14 of its prisons. In seven other states, including Washington and New Mexico, cottages, trailers, mobile homes, even tents are used.

Washington State's David Jirovec hired two hit men to kill his wife for insurance money. Now serving a life sentence, the Walla Walla inmate receives conjugal visits from his new wife. In New Mexico, it took a public uproar to cancel Ricky Abeyta's eligibility for that state's program after he married in prison. Abeyta had killed seven people, including two police officers and a five-month-old baby.

According to Larry Meachum, Connecticut's Commissioner of Correction, "We must attempt to modify criminal behavior and hopefully not return a more damaged human being to society than we received." It's a statement repeated over and over by prison administrators as the reason for the vast array of recreational and physical-fitness amenities available to convicts.

Weight-lifting equipment, all but universal in prisons, is far more expensive than most taxpayers might suspect. The Arizona Department of Corrections, for example, calculated that injuries sustained by prisoners lifting weights produced medical bills of $600,000 to $700,000 in 1993 in that state alone.

At the high-security Sullivan prison in Fallsburg, N.Y., twin yards filled with barbells and recreational equipment also have outdoor TVs, so inmates working out don't miss their favorite shows. Inside, prisoners "jam" in a music room crammed with electric guitars, amplifiers, drums and keyboards.

In Pennsylvania, most felons can get in-cell cable TV, including premium channels, at a huge discount. The maximum-security federal penitentiary at Lewisburg, Pa., offers Home Box Office and Cinemax to its resident drug dealers and killers.

At the Jefferson City Correctional Center in Missouri, inmates run their own around-the-clock, closed-circuit TV studio. Four channels routinely broadcast movies containing sex, horror and violence.

Hollywood likes to film at the century-old State Correctional Institution in Pittsburgh because it looks like a real prison: massive stone walls, guard towers and a huge core building with five ugly tiers of barred cells. But inmates can wander the yard at will, congregate in gangs, lounge on the steps of buildings.

Visitors enter the prison in large numbers, and contraband—including drugs—is a big problem. "Security has become a costly nightmare," complains a state prison employee.

Socializing with the outside world is also a feature of prison life. In Louisiana, the Angola prison Drama Club players (whose president is a convicted murderer) visit colleges and theaters. On the grounds of the Penitentiary of New Mexico near Santa Fe, some 1200 inmates and their guests whoop it up at the annual "Outta Joint" picnic. At the 1993 festivities, they were entertained by a clown, a puppet show, a political-satire performance and eight bands.

On March 19, 1994, in the $2-million visitors' center at the Massachusetts Correctional Institution in Norfolk, the Lifers Group held its annual "Lifers Banquet." Some 33 convicts, mostly murderers, and 49 invited guests enjoyed catered prime-rib dinners.

Reprinted by permission of Pat McCarthy and Creators Syndicate.

"Inmates are sent here *as* punishment, but not *for* punishment," says Joseph T. Smith, Deputy Superintendent for Programs at Bedford Hills Correctional Facility, a maximum-security prison in New York State. In truth, nothing seems too much for society's predators.

How did the pendulum swing so far from the austere, even harsh, conditions of the past? John J. DiIulio, a prominent political scientist at Princeton University who has studied and written about America's prisons for 15 years, explains: "Prisons used to emphasize inmate discipline and forced labor, and wardens ruled the cellblocks with an iron fist. Beginning in the 1960s, federal courts stepped in. At first, judges ruled only that prisoners were entitled to nutritious meals, basic health services and protection against arbitrary discipline at the hands of guards. But a number of federal judges went well beyond such reasonable reforms and began ordering that prisoners be provided with expensive, untested treatment programs and a wide range of recreational opportunities regardless of the cost.

"Most of these judges never set foot inside prison themselves," DiIulio continues. "Instead they appointed monitors to investigate prison conditions—many of whom came from the prison-rights movement. At first, security-minded wardens resisted the new orders from federal judges. But their resistance was gradually undercut by case managers and psychiatric social workers. In time, treatment personnel became top prison officials.

"When many prisons experienced unprecedented numbers of escapes and had hostage-taking incidents," adds DiIulio, "the remaining guards from the old school argued that discipline had become too lax. But nobody listened, preferring instead to hear academic 'experts' proclaim that prison violence and other problems were caused by a lack of adequately funded rehabilitation programs. More programs, of course, mean bigger staffs, fatter budgets and more perks."

In principle, few Americans would oppose basic efforts to educate and rehabilitate convicts. But what we have today borders on the absurd.

Morgan County Regional Correctional Facility in Tennessee offers six vocational programs and four levels of academic education. To house the expanding programs, it had to erect a new education building at a cost of $1.5 million. In California the corrections budget for 1993–94 includes $50 million for academic education, $40 million for vocational training and $57 million for inmate employment.

In 1993, the Boston *Globe* reported, Massachusetts set up a Correction Recovery Academy in its state prisons, at a price tag of $1000 per inmate. A major component was yoga.

At the Dade Correctional Institution near Miami, members of the Inmates' Cultural Club have developed a taste for opera. Prison librarian Rolando Valdes obtained a series of federal grants and purchased a 50-inch television and laser-disc equipment. Each Saturday night, he conducts opera appreciation classes in the prison library. Funded by another government grant, several inmates have even written their own opera, *El Caido*—a tale of a prisoner who rehabilitates himself. Says co-composer Elton Edwards, a "lifer" convicted of murdering a homeowner during a robbery, "It's been great therapy for us."

Therapy for mental health, aggressive behavior, domestic violence, sex offenses and substance abuse has grown into a prison cottage industry. Yet, after decades of attempting behavior modification, the overall results of rehabilitation and therapy are meager. When asked by *Reader's Digest* how many sex offenders he has rehabilitated in his years on the job, one New York State prison counselor bluntly responded, "None."

Inmates, for their part, are not fools: participation in education and therapy can chip time off their terms. "The saying among inmates is 'get a program,'" says criminologist Charles Logan of the University of Connecticut. "They know that it will help with the parole board."

Studies by the U.S. Bureau of Justice Statistics have shown that between 60 and 70 percent of inmates revert to crime after release. A model federal prison at Butner, N.C., applied every known rehabilitation technique to inmates for over a decade. The results: no reduction in recidivism and no improvement in convicts' employment prospects.

After extensive study of prison rehabilitation, criminologist Logan concludes: "Despite claims to the contrary, no type of treatment has been effective in rehabilitating criminals or preventing future criminal behavior."

At present, prisons or prison systems in 35 states operate under federal court order. In North Carolina, following a class-action lawsuit brought by state inmates, U.S. District Court Judge James B. McMillan approved a settlement in which the state would provide, at each of 13 prisons, softball and basketball equipment for two teams, a piano, a set of drums, three guitars—and five Frisbees.

Elsewhere, prison inmates have demanded and won access to pornography. Says Pam Smith-Steward, a senior staff attorney for the California Department of Corrections, "One inmate, who tortured and killed his own infant daughter, wrote sadistic stories in exchange for pornographic photos of women being tortured. When the prison staff confiscated and destroyed the photos, he sued in federal court. California taxpayers ended up paying the prisoner compensation."

In 1993, inmates filed nearly 33,000 civil suits in federal courts—a stunning 14 percent of all federal civil lawsuits. The New York State Attorney General estimates that prisoner lawsuits chew up 20 percent of his department's resources. In Arizona, 70 percent of all lawsuits brought against the state are by prisoners.

And things are getting worse. In 1993 Congress passed the Religious Freedom Restoration Act (RFRA), intended to protect the religious freedoms of American citizens from government intrusion. But at the urgent request of 25 state attorneys general and the heads of every state prison system, Sen. Harry Reid (D., Nev.) introduced an amendment excluding prisoners from the law's strict provisions. State officials were certain that RFRA would allow inmates to file even more outrageous lawsuits.

Attorney General Janet Reno dismissed their concerns, however, and urged Congress "to approve the bill without amendment." Reid's amendment was defeated.

Indeed, RFRA has opened a Pandora's box. Following a "religious freedom" lawsuit, the Florida Department of Corrections has been forced to allow into state prisons virulently racist materials intended to incite hatred of whites. In Illinois, a follower of the "religious" arm of the Aryan Nation—which believes in exterminating blacks and Jews—has sued under RFRA to demand its own ministers, literature and the right to congregate inside prisons.

After adjusting for inflation, prison spending per inmate is nearly 2½ times higher than it was three decades ago. In fiscal 1994, prisons cost society around $20 billion. Says Princeton's DiIulio: "At least 40 percent of prison expenses go to rehabilitation programs and inmate amenities that have little bearing on institutional security, and that far exceed basic standards of human dignity. Roughly speaking, prisons cost nearly twice as much as they should."

When Sam Lewis took charge of the Arizona Department of Corrections in the mid-1980s, he found "security problems and a bunch of spoiled inmates." A former Airborne paratrooper, Lewis decided to clean house.

He has imposed a strict dress and grooming code and ordered that newly built prisons would have no weight-lifting equipment. He also stopped unescorted furloughs, interprison recreational travel and the annual prison rodeo. To alleviate overcrowding, he started double-bunking inmates in some maximum-security facilities and using inmate labor to build new prisons.

"The message inmates are supposed to get," Lewis explains, "is 'this is not a place I want to be'—not because it's brutal, but because it's a strict, tough environment without a lot of creature comforts." The results? The system's escape rate, once the highest in the nation, plummeted—and so did costs. Arizona now spends 38 percent less than the national average to build a new medium-security prison cell and 45 percent less for a maximum-security cell.

Arizona Governor Fife Symington has encouraged Lewis's reforms and become sharply critical of federal judges who interfere with prison operations. "It's nonsense for them to say that convicts have a Constitutional right to taxpayer-provided services that many taxpayers can't afford on their own," he declares.

"The intellectual and bureaucratic forces that have turned prisons into 'resorts' are deeply entrenched," John DiIulio notes. "They won't be changed unless there's a loud, persistent and politically pointed public outcry."

Until then, we will see memos such as the following, which was posted at the Massachusetts Correctional Institution in Norfolk by policy coordinator James Krantz: "A third softball field will be made in the West Field in order to allow more inmates to play softball. The horseshoe pits will be temporarily relocated near the golf course. The bocci area will be relocated at the site of the new gym. The soccer field will be relocated to the East Field behind the softball field."

Hasn't the time come for us to require public officials to explain why prisons need to be resorts?

> "If our prisons are such resorts, simply open the gates and see how many run out . . . and how many walk in."

PRISONS DO NOT CODDLE INMATES

Jon Marc Taylor

In the following viewpoint, Jon Marc Taylor disputes Robert James Bidinotto's viewpoint and calls it "a piece of dangerous distortion, careful omission and false information." Taylor, a contributing editor for *Prison Life* magazine, argues that America's prisons are not the "resorts" that Bidinotto claims they are. He maintains that prison conditions such as overcrowding are becoming worse and that inmates are inadequately educated and trained. In addition, the costs of prison services that Bidinotto objects to—including counseling, education, and training—constitute a small fraction of prison expenses, according to Taylor.

As you read, consider the following questions:

1. What factors regarding Pennsylvania's prison system did Robert James Bidinotto omit from his viewpoint, according to Taylor?
2. According to Taylor, what percentage of California's 1993–94 corrections budget went to prisoner education?
3. How did a Scandinavian commission describe America's prison system, according to the author?

Jon Marc Taylor, "Lies About 'Resort' Prisons," *Prison Life*, July/August 1995. Reprinted by permission of the publisher.

> Those who corrupt the public mind are just as evil as those who steal from the public purse.
>
> Adlai Stevenson

In 1994, the Mississippi legislature met in special session to deal with the overcrowding of its prison system. (The entire Mississippi system is under federal court order to improve conditions of confinement.) Instead, the august assembly decided to confiscate prisoners' TVs, ban air-conditioning and weight-lifting equipment and dress their prisoners in striped uniforms with CONVICT stenciled across the back. Throughout the country, politicians, such as New York State Senator Michael Nozzolio, pontificate that "we have too many benefits and too little punishment" in our prisons.

Fueling the largely one-sided election-year diatribes were press reports, such as Robert Bidinotto's editorially trumpeted "Must Our Prisons Be Resorts?" in the November 1994 issue of *Reader's Digest*. The author claimed to have visited 14 institutions and interviewed officials at dozens of others. Bidinotto wrote of the cushy conditions and the mollycoddling of prisoners in inflammatory language and took an approach that was far from objective.

BLATANT PROPAGANDA

Overall, Bidinotto's article is a piece of dangerous distortion, careful omission and false information, reflecting a rigorous one-dimensional point of view. Except for the outright lies, which the quoted experts uttered for him, his article is a classic case of Goebbelian propaganda, a pernicious twist on reality circulated to 28 million homes. The article is a good example of why only 13 percent of the respondents in a 1994 Harris Poll said they had a "great deal of confidence" in the news reported by the press.

Bidinotto begins the article by describing the good life at Pennsylvania's Mercer Regional Correctional Facility. He expresses amazement and disgust at the recreational facilities, the psychological counseling and the basically civil treatment prisoners there receive. What Bidinotto failed to report was that the facility was one of the newest in a state system that in 1990 was on the verge of collapse. In 1993, Pat McManus, then prison commissioner, testified in a statewide trial on prison conditions that "overcrowding, in combination with idleness, is a formula for disaster."

That disaster in progress in the late 1980s and early 1990s led to riots and prison lockdowns throughout a prison system that is crammed to 170 percent capacity. The violent and expensive Camp Hill prison riot of 1989 exemplified the serious problems and inhumane conditions found in the Pennsylvania prison system.

Five weeks into a federal trial convened after the riot, during which prisoner after prisoner testified to inadequately investigated and rarely punished guard brutality and excessive force, the state of Pennsylvania entered into an 87-page settlement to improve living conditions, health care and job and education opportunities. All of these contextual factors were conveniently omitted in the *Reader's Digest* article.

The most distorted allegation made in the article was that the 160-year-old Missouri State Prison (rechristened Jefferson City Correctional Center) is a resort. This is a state penal system bulging at 160 percent capacity, where prisoners are forced to sleep in converted kitchens and where portable toilets are trucked in to meet the demand, a system where barely one percent of the overall budget is used for education and vocational training. Bidinotto's claim of cushy conditions stemmed from the fact that the prison has an inmate-operated around-the-clock closed-circuit TV studio that broadcasts "movies containing sex, horror and violence." But to the prisoners at Jefferson City, who must endure roach-infested cells, barely edible food and a health care system so lacking that prisoners liken a serious illness to a drawn-out death sentence, Bidinotto's focusing solely on the prisoner broadcast system totally misses the mark.

JeffTown's Broadcast Success

"JeffTown" (the name of the closed-circuit system) is a communication/entertainment network completely funded by the profits from items prisoners purchase from the commissary. It is watched on prisoner-bought TVs. The percentage of R, PG and G-rated films shown on the system match the ratio of similarly rated films released each year by Hollywood, and are no more violent or sexual than those available at the neighborhood Blockbuster.

In addition to funding the cable system and user fees, Jeff-Town weekly rebroadcasts over a hundred hours of educational, PBS and religious programs, another key point omitted from the article. Periodically, the superintendent uses the system to talk directly to the 2,000-man population, and on one occasion credited JeffTown's service with helping him calm the institution after a major disturbance, thereby avoiding further costly trouble. Beyond the mere entertainment value, Earl Fleer, the system's chief technician and newscaster, comments that "Jeff-Town serves a very needed and useful purpose."

With the recording and studio equipment, the JeffTown staff has produced several high-quality video programs. One video was a sales/production tape on the institution's shoe factory, which helped secure sales to other correctional systems. Other shows have included prisoner-featured substance abuse/recovery stories, one of which has been copied over 400 times and shown by many public and private organizations in Arizona, Washington, Colorado, Kansas and Missouri.

Moreover, JeffTown provides production facilities for other state agencies that simply cannot afford the $10,000 production fee that the standard one-hour video costs on the streets. Jeff-Town's additional benefit is the certified vocational training its technicians receive.

The final interesting twist to the JeffTown story is that no one, from the superintendent on down to the video technicians, was ever contacted by anyone from *Reader's Digest*. The information provided in the story, as brief as it was, must have come from secondary sources.

A Serious Omission

Of all the selective examples, half-truths and glaring omissions in the piece, perhaps the most serious was the citation regarding the corrections budget in California. Bidinotto intimated that the $50 million allocated for education and the $40 million for vocational training was a ridiculously generous sum, and that the $57 million for prisoner employment was an outright waste of taxpayers' money.

What we were not told was that the 1993–94 budget for the California Department of Corrections (CDC) was nearly $3.2 billion. Nor were we told that the combined education expenditures accounted for less than three percent of the overall budget. Further, the article failed to mention that two-thirds of prisoners have not graduated from high school, nearly the same number lived below the poverty line before their incarceration and almost half were employed only part-time before their arrest.

With education and training, two of the few rehabilitative measures that have proven successful, it is true, as Bidinotto states, that "what we have borders on the absurd." What is absurd, though, is that of every dollar spent on corrections, only three cents goes to education and training. The absurdity is not the amount of money spent on such programs, but why so little is invested in the first place.

The most contrived implication in the article was that the $57 million spent on California prisoner employment is a waste. What most Americans don't realize is that the vast majority of prisoner labor is either for necessary institutional services (i.e. food service, laundry, janitorial work) or factory work that produces a profit for the state. At the average wage of 15 cents an hour, divided into $57 million and multiplied by the average California C.O. wage of $16 an hour, if prisoner labor was replaced with state employees, the $57 million would cost taxpayers $6 billion.

Not only does prison employment provide inmates with something to do, and with some pocket change to buy medication the prison no longer provides free, it enables the state to purchase labor at one one-hundredth the cost of freeworld rates. How much slavery does it take to please Bidinotto and the editors at Reader's Digest?

The "Experts"

Throughout the article, two experts, professors John DiIulio of Princeton University and Charles Logan of the University of Connecticut, were repeatedly cited to lend their "expert analysis" of the luxurious and wasteful state of American prisons. The only problem was that their information was wrong and their political/professional agendas were hidden.

Professor DiIulio, in large brush strokes, painted the evolution of prison conditions from one of "discipline and forced labor, where wardens rul[ed] cellblocks with an iron fist" to the easy and cushy circumstances prisoners find themselves in today. He attributes this to prisoner lawsuits, misdirected court orders and liberal consent decrees. "At first," reports DiIulio, "security-minded wardens resisted the new orders from federal judges. But their resistance was gradually undercut by case managers and psychiatric social workers. In time, treatment personnel became top prison officials.

"When many prisons experienced unprecedented numbers of escapes and had hostage-taking incidents," DiIulio continues, "the remaining guards from the old school argued that discipline had become too lax. But nobody listened, preferring instead to hear academic 'experts' proclaim that prison violence and other problems were caused by a lack of adequately funded rehabilitation programs. More programs, of course, mean bigger staffs, fatter budgets and more perks."

This is a distorted picture, drawn from a few extreme cases, which in no way reveal the results caused by overcrowding without corresponding increases in staffing. Moreover, treatment staff did not "gain control." As Dr. Manoucheher Khatibi, the director of the Youthful Offender Program Office for the Florida Department of Corrections, comments: "Current correctional practice often places education (i.e. treatment) programs at the bottom of the heap in terms of priority." And since the number of successful escapes and prison violence have decreased over the past decade, the allegation that custody has lost its grip is simply not true.

The *Reader's Digest* article goes on to state that corrections cost the country around $20 billion in 1994. DiIulio claims that "at least 40 percent of prison expenses go to rehabilitation programs and inmate amenities that have little bearing on institutional security, and that far exceed basic standards of human dignity."

Notice, though, how Bidinotto failed to mention that the U.S. spent upwards of $25 billion on prison construction and operations, and the way he defines amenities: "Those small but valued things one does not expect but is pleased to discover in prison, such as hot coffee, tasty food or clean sheets."

With education, vocational training, drug treatment and counseling taking up a mere seven percent of penal expenditures, are we to believe that such precious few "amenities" as hot java and edible meals (real luxuries, those) consume a third of the national correctional budget?

FALLACIES BY GET-TOUGH THEORISTS

Since the publication of his 1987 book, *Governing Prisons: A Comparative Study of Correctional Management*, DiIulio has advocated a "control-oriented" prison regime of strict order, with some services and earned amenities. Arguably, then, if one doesn't follow the rules, no hot coffee or clean bedding. One can surmise that the film "Shawshank Redemption" depicts what the professor believes prison should be.

Looking more closely at this expert, we learn that DiIulio's mentor is Dr. James Q. Wilson, the godfather of the get-tough movement advocating judicial restraint, mandatory incarcerations, longer sentences and the abolishment of parole boards, to mention just a few of the principles that have governed criminal justice policy in America for the past 20 years. With teachers like that, no wonder the Princeton professor sees the world through concrete and barbed wire.

The other expert, Professor Charles Logan, did not lament plush prison conditions. Instead, he slammed correctional programming as a waste of time and money, and as an opportunity for con-wise prisoners to manipulate the system. "Despite claims to the contrary," Logan observes, "no type of treatment has been effective in rehabilitating criminals or preventing future criminal behavior."

This claim is most certainly false. In fact, in another of DiIulio's tomes, NO ESCAPE: The Failure of American Corrections (1991), the author concludes after reviewing the compendium of research (presumably the same reports Logan studied) that "the facile notion that 'nothing works' [in rehabilitation programming] is ready for the garbage heap of correctional history." Well structured, adequately supported programs, from education to vocational training to counseling, can and do help reduce crime and reincarceration rates.

THE REAL PROBLEM IS WAREHOUSING

The claim that our prisons are country clubs is ludicrous. The so-called country club prison has been likened [by Robert B. Levinson] to "the Loch Ness monster—many people believe in it but nobody has ever seen one." Although it is true that some prisons offer comforts, these generally are modest. The real problem often is warehousing—the storage of inmates in penal environments that offer them little or nothing constructive to do.

Robert Johnson, Corrections Today, July 1996.

Logan, on the other hand, has built his academic reputation on his get-tough theory of crime control. After two decades of the implementation of that concept and its dismal failure, one concludes that the author must be professionally desperate to try to salvage something from this obvious fallacy.

Canadian criminologists Paul Gendreau and Robert Ross reviewed two decades of research regarding deterrence theory policies and programs. They could not find "a single study in the whole deterrence literature which could support a cause-effect conclusion." Whereas Ross, in reviewing the effectiveness of just prison college programming, concluded that "nowhere in the literature can one find such impressive results with the recidivistic adult offender."

Yet, we already know, after Congress expelled prisoners from the Pell Grant program, that no matter how effective higher education opportunities ultimately are for society in general, they are just too damn luxurious for prisoners.

A decade ago, former U.S. Supreme Court Chief Justice Warren Burger said: "If anyone is tempted to regard humane prison reform as 'coddling' criminals, let him visit a prison and talk with inmates and staff. I have visited some of the best and some of the worst prisons and have never seen signs of coddling, but I have seen the terrible results of the boredom and frustration of empty hours and pointless existence."

Since then, conditions have only grown worse, not better. As a whole, the U.S. prison system is in violation of the Universal Declaration of Human Rights and the International Convention on Civil and Political Rights. Recently, a Scandinavian commission found the American prison system to be "the most barbarous" among the Western industrialized countries.

No, the nation's prisons are far from resorts. Claims that they are resorts are nothing more than attempts to mislead the public from the real ills troubling society. Why, if per capita crime is the lowest it has been in 20 years, are prisons still expanding? Why, if unemployment is at a relatively low level (job security notwithstanding), are real family incomes still shrinking? Why are we being told that if we just had tougher prisons instead of more equitable economic opportunities, crime would all but disappear? Answers to these questions would reveal a criminal philosophy that dwarfs all the exploitation found in our prisons.

If our prisons are such resorts, simply open the gates and see how many run out . . . and how many walk in.

PERIODICAL BIBLIOGRAPHY

The following articles have been selected to supplement the diverse views presented in this chapter. Addresses are provided for periodicals not indexed in the *Readers' Guide to Periodical Literature*, the *Alternative Press Index*, the *Social Sciences Index*, or the *Index to Legal Periodicals and Books*.

Holly J. Burkhalter — "Torture in U.S. Prisons," *Nation*, July 3, 1995.

Ronald Burns — "Boot Camps: The Empirical Record," *American Jails*, July/August 1996. Available from American Jail Association, 2053 Day Rd., Suite 100, Hagerstown, MD 21740-9795.

Stephen J. Ingley — "It's the Wave of the Past: Getting Tough (Nasty) on Criminals," *American Jails*, September/October 1995.

Robert Johnson — "Humane Prisons: A Call for Decency in Conservative Times," *Corrections Today*, July 1996.

Nan D. Miller — "International Protection of the Rights of Prisoners: Is Solitary Confinement in the United States a Violation of International Standards? *California Western International Law Journal*, Fall 1995.

Robert Perkinson — "Shackled Justice: Florence Federal Penitentiary and the New Politics of Punishment," *Social Justice*, Fall 1994.

Ricardo Ramirez — "Prison Reform and the Ideals of Justice," *Origins*, March 2, 1995.

Shep — "Control Unit Madness," *Z Magazine*, December 1994.

Margaret P. Spencer — "Sentencing Drug Offenders: The Incarceration Addiction," *Villanova Law Review*, February 1995.

Richard Stratton — "The End of Rehabilitation," *Prison Life*, October 1996. Available from PO Box 537, Stone Ridge, NY 12484.

Corey Weinstein — "Fighting the American Gulag," *Third Force*, January/February 1995. Available from Center for Third World Organizing, 1218 E. 21st St., Oakland, CA 94606.

Robert Worth — "A Model Prison," *Atlantic Monthly*, November 1995.

Chapter 3

Should Prisons Use Inmate Labor?

Chapter Preface

In 1984, Congress created the Prison Industry Enhancement Program to allow federal and state prisons to sell inmate-made products on the open market. Additionally, the program allowed private companies to contract with prisons for inmate labor. By 1996, more than seventy thousand inmates were working in prison industries, performing data entry, light manufacturing, printing, and other labor.

Proponents of prison labor programs argue that participating inmates learn work skills, earn money that helps pay for prison costs and victim restitution, and are less likely to commit crimes upon their release. According to the criminal justice reform organization Justice Fellowship, offenders, victims, government, and the community all benefit from inmate labor. In the words of the organization, "Prison industries should be required to employ as many inmates as possible so that the benefits will be as extensive as possible."

But critics contend that prison labor exploits inmates and harms businesses and workers. Many observers assert that the working conditions in most prisons are abysmal. California state prisoner and upholstery worker Willie Wisely maintains, "Unskilled prisoners teach other unskilled prisoners how to do the work" with unsafe machinery and in workspaces where the atmosphere is laced with hazardous particulate debris. Labor union and business leaders argue that inmates' low-cost labor depresses wages and deprives other workers of jobs. "We have to compete with prison labor making sixty cents an hour," apparel executive Doug Small complains.

Proponents applaud the billions of dollars generated annually by prisoners' products and services. But opponents assert that the exploitation of prisoners and the violation of their rights tarnishes the practice of prison labor. The authors in the following chapter present opposing views on whether prisons should use inmate labor.

"Allowing prisoners to work makes sense, especially when the work will make the streets safer."

INMATE LABOR IS BENEFICIAL

Pete du Pont

Former Delaware governor Pete du Pont is the policy chairman of the National Center for Policy Analysis in Washington, D.C. In the following viewpoint, du Pont argues that increasing the use of inmate labor in America would benefit prisoners, prisons, and society. He contends that prisons should use inmate labor to help pay for operating costs, as they did earlier in American history. The author maintains that inmates would also benefit from the skills acquired from prison labor, improving their ability to lead productive lives outside of prison.

As you read, consider the following questions:

1. According to du Pont, what percentage of inmates were involved in productive labor in 1885?
2. What is government's first responsibility, according to the author?
3. In du Pont's opinion, what factors could make inmate labor disadvantageous?

Pete du Pont, "Convicts in the Workplace?" This article appeared in the March 1996 issue and is reprinted with permission from the *World & I*, a publication of The Washington Times Corporation, ©1996.

Today's prison reformers might not agree with the eighteenth-century French prison reformer Jean-Jacques Vilain that "if any man will not work, neither let him eat." Still, in today's debates about how to finance needed prison space and reduce repeat visits to prison, we would do well to look to the past. History is usually an excellent teacher, and the history of prison work shows us that putting prisoners to work while behind bars is good not just for the prisoners but for society, as well.

LABOR FOR OPERATING COSTS

During the first century and a half of our nation's history, prisons earned a major part of their daily operating costs by leasing convict labor to private employers. As an indication of the benefits of such arrangements, proceeds from inmate labor at New York's Newgate Prison, opened in 1797, paid nearly all of the prison's expenses during its first five years of operation. The American Correctional Association notes that the prison wardens of those times were under substantial pressure to make their prisons financially self-sufficient and were "concerned as much about profits as prisoners."

Supporters of prison work at the time pointed to the fact that inmates received better vocational training and produced more income for the state. The practice was so beneficial and so accepted that, by 1885, three-fourths of prison inmates were involved in productive labor, the majority working for private employers under contract and leasing arrangements. There is no doubt that incarceration costs were reduced, and while the surviving evidence is less than overwhelming, at least some of it indicates that inmates who worked while in prison were less likely to return to prison upon their release.

PRISON LABOR DECLINES

Yet, by the 1930s, only 44 percent of prison inmates worked, and nearly all worked for state industries rather than for private employers. By 1984, just 16 percent of prisoners worked in manufacturing or farming, and by the time of the 1990 census, this number had fallen to 11 percent. What happened between the success of our nation's early history and today? During the Depression, 33 states passed laws prohibiting the sale of inmate-made goods in the open market. Congress enacted the Hawes-Cooper Act in 1929, which put a federal imprimatur on state provisions restricting inmate-made goods. While Hawes-Cooper was repealed in 1978, it had long since been superseded by the more restrictive Ashurst-Sumner Act of 1940, which made it a federal crime to knowingly transport inmate-made goods in interstate commerce.

Even states that did not go so far as to prohibit the sale of inmate-made goods, such as New York, adopted the "state-use" system, which permitted convicts to only manufacture goods for sale to governmental agencies. The "state-use" principle was not a complete ban, but it certainly resulted in a very limited market for convict labor. In 1936, Congress passed the Walsh-Healy Act, banning convict labor on federal contracts exceeding $10,000 in value.

THE BENEFITS OF PRISON LABOR

An estimated 90 percent of America's prisoners are unemployed, although the merits of prison labor are well established. A 1991 study by the U.S. Bureau of Prisons found that employed inmates are half as likely to commit crimes once released as unemployed inmates. Employed inmates are also more likely to find work after their release and to find better-paying jobs. . . .

Prison labor was effectively eliminated by federal statute 50 years ago at the behest of organized labor. Before then, the United States had a robust history of employing prisoners for menial farming and factory tasks. Early Americans supported prison labor because it provided operating revenue for prisons and because they thought it encouraged offenders' spiritual reformation. Work, it was believed, eliminated opportunities for inmates to get into trouble. Work gave them direction and ate up otherwise idle time, all the while demonstrating the fruits of productive labor. . . .

If prisoners are given the right incentives to work industriously, such as better living conditions or slightly reduced sentences, employers might once again invest in a population whose members are always on time for work and who can neither complain effectively nor quit. By deregulating prison labor and returning the issue to the states, Congress might well make prison labor as widespread and beneficial as it was when inmates were an important part of our economy—and, not coincidentally, when our streets were safer.

Andrew Peyton Thomas, *Weekly Standard*, March 4, 1996.

These statutes are a form of protectionism, designed to protect the providers of goods and services in the free market from having to compete with convict labor. Small businesses and labor unions continue to view such competition as unfair and have successfully prevented relaxation of the statutes. Even when

Congress tried to change the laws in 1979, the best it could do was to allow prisoner work only when those prisoners are paid the prevailing wage, labor unions approve, local labor is unaffected, and no local unemployment is produced. Not surprisingly with such onerous constraints, a mere 1,660 prisoners, out of 1 million, were working under these provisions in 1994.

As Andrew Peyton Thomas, the assistant attorney general of Arizona, notes in the March 30, 1995, *Wall Street Journal*,

> Prison labor, once viewed as indispensable for restoring a healthy relationship between the criminal and society, was made literally a federal offense. Instead of ceding certain jobs to prisoners to aid in their reformation . . . Americans sought crime control on the cheap. As it turned out, those jobs were eventually lost anyhow to lower-paid foreigners.

Time to Earn Their Keep

These developments are disappointing. Many prisoners are eager to work, if only to relieve the tedium of prison life. In addition to reduced incarceration costs, potential benefits include restitution to victims and the opportunity to provide family support while still in prison.

More important, the work is good for society in the long run because it reduces crime. Most people would agree that if prisoners learned a skill while they were in jail, they could more easily get a job when they left jail, and that an ex-prisoner with a job is less likely to commit another crime. Because nearly one-half of people released from prison return to jail within three years, job skills could mean a significant decline in the crime rate.

The only disadvantages of more work opportunities for prisoners are the feared competitive effects on local labor markets, but the government's first responsibility is to citizens, not to narrow interest groups. Besides, economic theory tells us that new production benefits all Americans, and the real world proves this theory by having prison production raise the demand for other services and create new goods for consumers to purchase.

It is no doubt true that while prison labor is good for our economy as a whole, it may place competitive pressures on individual firms or local labor. But that is not a valid reason to restrict prison work. It is time to dust off the historic English legal principle that competition is not a tort. The simple truth is that the fact that one person's production disadvantages another competitor is irrelevant. Operating in the marketplace is always fraught with a multitude of competitive risks, so why single out protection against just one of them? Competition is not a wrong to be righted. It is, rather, the strength of our economic system, so our policies should be to break down the barriers to prison work.

POPULAR PROGRAMS

The state of Washington has one of the most advanced prison industry programs in the country, with involvement from private companies. And while only 3% of the state's inmates are employed by private companies, the culture of work habits and work values is felt by other inmates. Income generated by these prisoners goes toward restitution payments to victims and helps offset room and board. Like other prison industries programs, inmate participation is voluntary and popular—often prisoners are put on waiting lists to participate. Washington state Secretary of Corrections Chase Riveland says that if the outdated regulatory barriers were lifted, half of his inmates could be employed. The impact on his institutions, he says, would be "revolutionary."

Edwin Meese III and Knut A. Rostad, *Wall Street Journal*, May 1, 1996.

The key element in the argument for knocking down the barriers erected over the last century and returning prison labor to the market is that, although prison work may be a form of competition, it is not a form of unfair competition. Profit is no more easily achieved in prison production than in free-market businesses. The potential advantage of the inexpensive cost of labor is offset by the disadvantage of lower productivity and the added costs of security, high turnover, lack of skills, lack of good work habits, and remote prison locations.

STEPS FOR THE RETURN OF PRISON WORK

So, what can we do to return the hum of productive work to our nation's prisons? We must begin by repealing state and federal limitations on inmate work, so that responsible private businesses can competitively bid for the use of prison labor and still have the opportunity to generate profits. Next, we must let prisons themselves "profit" from accepting these contracts and provide monetary incentives to wardens who lead their institutions to self-sufficiency.

Specifically, we must:
- Repeal state laws restricting markets for prison-made goods and services;
- Repeal the Ashurst-Sumner Act of 1940 so that inmate-produced goods can be transported across state lines;
- Repeal the Walsh-Healy Act prohibition on the use of in-

mate labor in federal procurement contracts in excess of $10,000;

- Repeal state and federal limitations on inmate pay to allow more flexible, market-determined wages (that is, wages linked to productivity); and
- Include measurements of progress toward prison self-sufficiency in wardens' personnel reviews.

It will not be easy for the private-sector bidders, because prison labor is not easy to use. Initially, the market value of prisoner labor will be very low, and the quality of their work will no doubt be poor, but both will improve as skills improve.

Allowing prisoners to work makes sense, especially when the work will make the streets safer for the rest of us. Across the country, a million prisoners are serving time in jail. Each month, 40,000 of them are released under mandatory supervision, on parole, or at the conclusion of their sentences. Our streets would be safer and the crime rate would be lower if these newly returned members of society had a skill, a job, and the beginning of a future.

| "The current [inmate labor] system certainly doesn't work, except for those who profit from prison labor."

INMATE LABOR MAY NOT BE BENEFICIAL

Reese Erlich

In the following viewpoint, Reese Erlich maintains that inmate labor programs exploit the prisoners. Erlich contends that the system he describes as the prison-industrial complex makes substantial profits from inmates' labor without providing them adequate work training to improve their skills and private employment prospects. In addition, the author argues, many union members' jobs are threatened because unions are unable to compete with inmates' cheap labor. Erlich is a former journalism lecturer at California State University in Hayward and a freelance reporter.

As you read, consider the following questions:

1. What are the three arrangements of prison labor, according to Erlich?
2. In Erlich's opinion, what change in the attitude toward prison labor occurred from the 1950s to the 1990s?
3. What may the prison-industrial complex lobby for in the future, in the author's opinion?

Reese Erlich, "Prison Labor: Workin' for the Man," *Covert Action Quarterly*, Fall 1995. Reprinted by permission of the author.

Convicted kidnapper Dino Navarrete doesn't smile much as he surveys the sewing machines at Soledad prison's sprawling workshop. The short, stocky man with tattoos rippling his muscled forearms earns 45 cents an hour making blue work shirts in a medium-security prison near Monterey, California. After deductions, he earns about $60 for an entire month of nine-hour days.

"They put you on a machine and expect you to put out for them," says Navarrete. "Nobody wants to do that. These jobs are jokes to most inmates here." California long ago stopped claiming that prison labor rehabilitates inmates. Wardens just want to keep them occupied. If prisoners refuse to work, they are moved to disciplinary housing and lose canteen privileges. Most importantly, they lose "good time" credit that reduces their sentence.

Navarrete was surprised to learn that California has been exporting prison-made clothing to Asia. He and the other prisoners had no idea that California, along with Oregon, was doing exactly what the U.S. has been lambasting China for—exporting prison-made goods. "You might just as well call this slave labor, then," says Navarrete. "If they're selling it overseas, you know they're making money. Where's the money going to? It ain't going to us." For the first time in the interview, Navarrete's usual scowl turned briefly into a smile.

Federal law prohibits domestic commerce in prison-made goods unless inmates are paid "prevailing wage." But because the law doesn't apply to exports, no California prison officials will end up in cells alongside their "employees."

SIMILAR ARGUMENTS

Interestingly enough, prison authorities on both sides of the Pacific make similar arguments to justify prison labor. "We want prisoners to learn a working skill," says Mai Lin Hua, warden at China's maximum security Shanghai Jail. He admits that his prisoners are forced to work, facing solitary confinement if they refuse. He also says China no longer exports prison-made goods to the U.S.

U.S. prison officials echo a similar line, except they claim the labor is voluntary. Fred Nichols, head of Oregon's "Prison Blues" jeans-making operation, says, "We provide extra training for them. Here the inmates volunteer."

But prisoners in Oregon, like those virtually everywhere else in the U.S., get time subtracted from their sentences for working in prison industries. If prisoners don't work, they serve longer sentences, lose privileges, and risk solitary confinement.

So what's the real difference between China's "forced labor" and that in the U.S. prison system? Brad Haga, marketing director for Oregon Prison Industries, sheepishly admits, "Perhaps it smacks of old-fashioned imperialism to be making those kinds of judgments."

A DYNAMIC SECTOR

Regardless of such qualms, hundreds of thousands of American prisoners now work in what is becoming a growth business: prison industries. The term encompasses several distinct but related arrangements: Federal and state prisons employ inmates to produce goods for sale to government and for the open market. Private companies as well contract with prisons to hire prisoners. And private prisons similarly employ inmate labor for private profit, either for outside companies or for the prison operators themselves. What all three arrangements share is the exploitation of a growing and literally captive labor pool.

And that pool is overflowing. The U.S. now has 1.12 million people behind bars, and its incarceration rate is second only to Russia's. The U.S. rate is more than four times Canada's, five times England's, and 14 times Japan's.

Some cite the country's violent traditions, chronic social tensions, and high crime rates to explain this perverse accomplishment. But such explanations beg the question of how society responds to crime and its causes. Instead of addressing the causes of criminality, political leaders and the mass media have inflamed popular concern about crime and sparked revulsion at notorious offenses. Hyped-up moral panics and crime hysteria lead to good ratings and easy political points. They also deflect attention from the causes of crime. The goal becomes simply to suppress deviance, a stance that prepares the terrain for a harshly repressive response to crime.

For those at the bottom, public policy has become all stick and no carrot. "Three strikes" and other mandatory minimum laws, the war on drugs, and moves to abolish parole are the concrete embodiments of the repressive approach. In the past 20 years, while serious crime rates have remained relatively stable, the incarceration rate has more than doubled. As programs for the poor and disadvantaged face the axe, spending for police and prisons grows rapidly.

As a result, U.S. prisons are jam-packed. To keep prisoners busy and increase revenues, prisons across the country are expanding prison industries. And conservative politicians are jumping on the bandwagon. Presidential candidate Sen. Phil

Gramm (R-Texas) has called for prison labor to pay half the cost of the federal prison system.

But beneath these pragmatic arguments lurks a darker subtext: the need to impose discipline and control over an ever-larger and increasingly restive prison population. Critics also charge that inmates are exploited, the jobs provide few real skills, and prison industries throw prisoners into direct competition with civilian workers.

RIPE FOR EXPLOITATION

In the 1950s, prison authorities, unions, and private companies reached a compromise on the issue of prison labor. The federal government and states agreed that prisoners should work as a means of rehabilitation. Inmate-produced goods would be used inside prisons or sold only to government agencies—and would not compete with private businesses or labor. Now, prison authorities, along with cost-conscious entrepreneurs, budget-paring politicians, and private prison operators such as Wackenhut and the Corrections Corporation of America (CCA), are in the process of overturning that long-held political consensus.

The law hasn't changed since the 1950s, but the political climate has moved so far to the right that it is often ignored. Nowadays, almost no one talks about rehabilitation. And in the go-go, free enterprise, let's-privatize-everything 1990s, many in authority just don't care if prison labor competes with civilians. Prisoners are one more sector ripe for exploitation.

In fact, some politicians and businesspeople view inmates much as they see workers in the Third World. In a revealing comment, Oregon State Representative Kevin Mannix argues that corporations should cut deals with prison systems just as Nike shoes does with the Indonesian government. Nike subcontractors there pay workers $1.20 per day. "We propose that [Nike] take a look at their transportation costs and their labor costs," says Mannix. "We could offer [competitive] prison inmate labor" in Oregon.

And prison labor is proving highly competitive. From 1980 to 1994, while the number of federal and state prisoners increased by 221 percent, the number of inmates employed in prison industries jumped by 358 percent. Prison industries sales have skyrocketed during those years from $392 million to $1.31 billion. And they're not just making license plates.

- Oregon prisoners sew jeans called "Prison Blues." Inmates are paid anywhere from 28 cents to $8.00/hour, but 80 percent of the higher wage is withheld.

- In 1994, a local prison secretly slipped Chicago-area prisoners into a Toys R Us store to stock shelves. Union protests stopped it.
- Southern California youth offenders book flights for TWA.
- Private companies hire prisoners in Ohio, California and other states to do data processing inside prisons.

THE PRISON-INDUSTRIAL COMPLEX

That prison labor is being exploited should come as no surprise. Prison industries are only one source of potential profits for companies feeding off the imprisonment boom. Prisons themselves are a growth industry. Federal, state, and local governments spent an estimated $30 billion for their prison systems in 1994, up from only $4 billion in 1975. In 1995, for the first time in its history, California spent more for prisons than on higher education.

"Prison construction is going crazy all over the country," one happy contractor told the New York Times. California officials estimate they will have to build 20 new prisons to handle the state's "three strikes" law. Florida plans eight new prisons and four new work camps by 2000. And, incredibly enough, Texas plans to open one new facility a week from 1995 to 1997. Larry Solomon, vice president of Joy Food Service in Florida, said sales to prisons are "a great, great business. Sales are just about doubling every year."

Corporate interest in prisons goes beyond construction and providing candy bars. Long distance phone carriers are falling all over themselves to provide pay phones to prisons. In return for the pay phone monopoly, they routinely kick back part of their profits to prison systems in the form of commissions. Why? Prisoners must phone collect, and the companies can charge substantially higher rates than at other pay phones.

A single prison phone can gross $15,000 per year, five times more than a street phone box. One of the worst offenders among the phone companies, RCNA, holds the contract for the Immigration and Naturalization Service (INS) detention center in Florence, Arizona. RCNA charges inmates $22 for a 15-minute call to the East Coast, with INS taking a 35 percent cut. The relatives paying for the calls often have no idea of the scam, until their phone bill comes.

NEW CORPORATE PLAYERS

Since the early 1980s, some new corporate players have joined the fray. Private companies such as CCA and Wackenhut are now building and operating private prisons under contract from federal and state governments. As of 1995, 13 states had private prisons.

CCA co-founder T. Don Hutto, a former Virginia corrections commissioner who jumped to the private sector, is but one example of a revolving door in corrections that has nothing to do with the recidivism rate. The interlocking directorates of former government officials and corporate boards looks alarmingly like the more familiar military-industrial version.

A CORPORATE WELFARE SCHEME

Convict labor is essentially a gigantic corporate welfare scheme: costs are socialized and only companies tied into the prison-industrial complex profit. Competing enterprises and workers lose.

Imprisoned workers have virtually no bargaining power with their employers, ensuring below-market wages. In some cases, employers simply replace their entire workforce with forced labor; in 1994, for example, Lockhart Technologies closed its circuit board assembly plant near Austin, Texas, laying off 150 employees, and moved the entire operation into a nearby prison.

Jesse Walker, Liberty, July 1996.

Wackenhut most strongly reflects this trend. Its board of directors includes former Marine Corps Commandant Paul X. Kelley, a pair of retired Air Force generals and a former Air Force under secretary, former Attorney General Benjamin Civiletti, and the former chair of AlliedSignal, among others.

But Wackenhut's competitors can play the game as well. When Esmor Correctional Services Corporation wanted to win a halfway house contract with the City of New York, it hired an aide to Democratic state Rep. Edolphus Towns. Both Towns and the aide had initially opposed the project.

Esmor also runs jails for the INS, so it made a senior vice president out of Richard Staley, a former acting INS director. And former acting Attorney General Stuart Gerson sits on Esmor's board of directors. These government ties didn't help Esmor, however, when INS detainees rebelled over bad conditions and almost destroyed its private prison in New Jersey.

This new prison-industrial complex is establishing a network of political contacts and local constituencies—wardens, prison guard unions, subcontractors and suppliers, and local government officials—that benefit from increased incarceration. As in the case of the prison pay phones, that complex will make great profits at the expense of the inmates and the public. Just as the country now struggles to get rid of unnecessary military bases and weapons systems, in the years ahead, the prison-industrial complex may lobby to maintain unneeded prisons or promote laws that help fill them.

WACKENHUT'S BRAVE NEW WORLD

For a glimpse of the future just visit the small town of Lockhart, Texas. Located about 30 miles outside Austin, the sleepy little town is most famous for a lip-smacking barbeque restaurant. But just down the road is a private prison run by Wackenhut. The private security firm in recent years has branched out and is now the second largest private prison operation in the U.S. And it's the very model of the prison-industrial complex.

Scott Comstock, warden at the Lockhart Work Program Facility, sits in a comfortably appointed office with an entire wall of deer and elk heads mounted behind him. He's been hunting for years, almost as long as he's been in the prison business. Comstock, as is the style in these parts, sports a mustache, Stetson hat, and cowboy boots. As an early member of the prison-industrial complex, he worked his way up from guard to warden in the Texas state system and then made the leap to the private sector.

"I think that Texas, in particular, has proven that privatization is a viable alternative," he says. And certainly, that arrangement has been viable for Wackenhut, which receives $31 per day per prisoner from the state. From that money, Comstock must provide housing, guards, electricity and everything else to run the facility. Whatever is left over is profit. So Comstock says adding prison industries to the mix can eventually help the bottom line.

At the moment, however, Wackenhut must convince private employers they will profit from locating in a prison. The Lockhart facility currently houses three private companies: Lockhart Technologies, Inc. (LTI) (circuit board assembly), a subsidiary of Ft. Lauderdale's United Vision Group (eyeglass manufacture) and Chatleff Controls (valves and fittings).

Leonard Hill, owner of LTI, is an unassuming man with thinning grey hair. He wears a sweater with no tie and appears shy and uncomfortable at the prospect of being interviewed. He is exactly the kind of small entrepreneur that prison industries are attracting across the country—not so big he can locate overseas, but not so small as to go belly up in the first months of operation. And in order to attract businesses like his, Wackenhut arranged a sweetheart deal that defense contractors could only dream about.

LTI, which assembles and repairs circuit boards for companies such as IBM, Dell, and Texas Instruments, got a completely new factory assembly room, built to specifications by prison labor. It pays only $1/year rent and gets a tax abatement from the city to boot. Hill closed his circuit board assembly plant in Austin, laid off 150 workers and moved all the equipment to Lockhart, where he pays prisoners minimum wage, as required by federal law. The prison then takes about 80 percent of inmate wages for room and board, victim restitution and other fees. Wackenhut argues this work benefits both the prisoners and society. But Hill is no do-gooding liberal out to help inmates. He made a hard-headed business decision to relocate inside the prison because he eventually expects to rake in bigger profits.

"Normally when you work in the free world," says Hill, "you have people call in sick, they have car problems, they have family problems. We don't have that here." Hill says the state pays for workers' compensation and medical care. And, he notes, inmates "don't go on vacations."

UNION LABOR AND PRISON LABOR

Under federal law, Wackenhut was supposed to consult with local businesses and unions before allowing LTI to set up shop. But the Texas AFL-CIO [American Federation of Labor and Congress of Industrial Organizations] was never consulted, according to its president, Joe Gunn. Gunn too sports a huge Stetson and has a penchant for string ties held together with a silver clasp in the shape of Texas. But Gunn is no mirror image of Warden Comstock.

Wackenhut violated the law by not consulting with labor, he charges, "and we're going to pursue it." He calls this kind of prison labor "absolute indentured slavery. [Wackenhut] puts people to work under conditions that we criticize China for."

Wackenhut denies any violation of the law, saying it followed guidelines established by the Texas Employment Commission (TEC), the state agency regulating such matters. But the TEC's guidelines follow a rather crabbed interpretation of federal law. The TEC claims Wackenhut needed to consult with unions only in the county where the plant was set up. Since there are no electronic unions in largely rural Caldwell County where Lockhart is located, Wackenhut had no one with whom to consult.

The Texas AFL-CIO begs to differ. The TEC should have required Wackenhut to consult with the AFL-CIO office in Austin in neighboring Travis County, where 150 jobs were lost, says Gunn.

The experience of the Texas AFL-CIO and the laid-off Austin

workers explains why the trade union movement has been among the most active opponents of private prisons and prison labor in general. In a few cases, unions have successfully fought prison industries. United Auto Workers (UAW) union members were shocked when they learned that Weastec Corporation in Ohio hired prisoners to assemble Honda parts. The company paid the state $2.05 an hour for inmate labor. From that, the prisoners got 35 cents an hour.

UAW Region 2 Director Warren Davis says the deal threatened union jobs even more than cheap parts imported under NAFTA [the North American Free Trade Agreement]. "No smaller employer could compete for that contract with Honda," says Davis.

Crying foul, the UAW Community Action Program contacted local legislators, other unions, and the media. State Rep. Rocco Colonna successfully sponsored bills in the Ohio House of Representatives banning prison industries from taking over civilian jobs. Although the legislation never passed the state senate, the pressure forced Honda to eliminate the prison labor contract in 1992.

"Honda backed off," says Davis, "because they didn't feel the negative publicity was worth it.". . .

DEAD END SKILLS?

Derek Hervey is serving a 15-year sentence for drug dealing. The slightly built African American is dressed in the green uniform worn by all LTI "employees." He says field work at the state-operated medium-security Sugarland prison was "hot, hard work, very abusive." At Lockhart, he got some basic education and works in a clean, air conditioned plant. (The air conditioning is for the circuit boards, not the men.) He hopes to get a job after release, noting that many companies in Texas manufacture circuit boards. "It's something I can apply for."

But the direct skills learned at LTI aren't going to get Hervey or anyone else a job. Owner Hill admits that most circuit board assemblers on the outside are immigrant women. "I think those people are not going to get jobs identical to what we're doing here," he admits. . . .

The current system certainly doesn't work, except for those who profit from prison labor. As long as the U.S. remains hellbent on packing the prisons, meaningful work programs that actually prepare inmates for life on the outside are worth a try. Otherwise, prisoners may as well be making license plates.

| "There appears to be no valid reason why states wishing to operate chain gangs as a part of the corrections program should not do so."

INMATE CHAIN GANGS ARE A PROPER FORM OF PUNISHMENT

Richard Lee Morris

In the following viewpoint, Richard Lee Morris argues that there is no valid reason for states not to utilize inmate chain gangs. The U.S. Constitution and Supreme Court have provided a legal foundation for states to use chain gangs, he contends. Morris maintains that chain gangs are justified as a deterrent to crime, as fitting punishment, and as a method to keep prisoners orderly. Morris is a graduate of the University of Alabama School of Law in Tuscaloosa.

As you read, consider the following questions:

1. How are inmates assigned to chain gangs, according to Morris?
2. According to the author, what does the Thirteenth Amendment recognize?
3. What advantages of road cleaning by chain gangs does Morris note?

From Richard Lee Morris, "Chain Gangs: A Proper Corrections Tool?" *Law and Psychology Review*, Spring 1996. Reprinted with permission.

A recent NBC television poll found that Americans were un-happy with the condition of the prison system in their country. The poll found that 82% of Americans believe prison life is too easy and more than 60% believe prison rehabilitation programs have failed. This mood has been evidenced by many changes in American prisons as well as in many proposed changes. In short, it seems that Americans are ready to get tough on criminals.

Many states have set out to make their prisons tougher. Alabama has reinstituted chain gangs, allows no cable television in its prisons, and forbids indoor smoking. Alabama also denies television, radio, telephone, and visitation privileges to those serving on chain gangs. Florida plans to reinstitute chain gangs, allows no more early releases, has cut off funds to replace prison televisions and recreational equipment, requires inmates to pay a fee for nonemergency medical care, requires inmates to shave, and requires inmates to wear military-style haircuts. Florida has also banned telephones from death row. Georgia has banned to-bacco in its prisons, forbidden its inmates from wearing beards or long hair, and does not provide air conditioning in its pris-ons. Georgia has also established inmate road crews and re-stricted the telephone and mail privileges of problem inmates. Mississippi, Virginia, Tennessee, South Carolina, North Carolina, and Michigan have all adopted similar "get tough" policies. Likewise, Arizona has begun to place inmates on chain gangs. Additionally, chain gangs have been proposed in Kansas, Wis-consin, and Kentucky. . . .

CHAIN GANG PROFILES

Those currently serving on chain gangs in Alabama work twelve hours per day. They are denied visitation privileges and pre-vented from watching television or listening to the radio. In-mates on Alabama chain gangs work primarily along the high-ways of the state. However, some work busting rocks. Road cleaning seems to be the typical type of work performed by chain gangs across the country. Chain gang members wear shackles and chains on their legs while they work and are guarded by armed personnel.

Inmates usually are assigned to chain gangs after volunteering for the work as an alternative to receiving some type of punish-ment for misbehaving in prison. However, some prisoners are assigned to chain gangs because they are repeat offenders or be-cause a judge has determined that it would be better for a par-ticular inmate to serve on the chain gang for a relatively short period of time, rather than serving a longer traditional sentence.

Understanding the type of work performed by chain gangs and the way in which an inmate is chosen for chain gang service should facilitate a basic understanding of modern chain gang operations. With this understanding in hand, the next step in determining whether the chain gang is a proper corrections tool is to focus on the substantive issues involved in the chain gang debate.

CONSTITUTIONAL CONCERNS

Are modern chain gangs prohibited by the United States Constitution? The answer to that question is not a simple one. In fact, there may be no definite answer. Clearly, there are constitutional prohibitions against cruel and unusual punishment and involuntary servitude. On its face, the constitutional prohibition against involuntary servitude provides an exception for those being punished for crimes of which they have been convicted. Likewise, the United States Supreme Court has stated that "[t]here can be no doubt that . . . [a state] . . . has authority to impose involuntary servitude as a punishment for crime." The Thirteenth Amendment, therefore, appears to present no obstacle to the operation of modern chain gangs. However, the constitutional prohibition against cruel and unusual punishment presents a more difficult issue.

A basic tenet of Anglo-Saxon jurisprudence is that citizens should not have inflicted upon them punishments which are disproportionate to the crimes they commit. Roots of this tenet can be found in the Magna Carta of 1215, which prohibited excessive fines. In 1689, the English Bill of Rights provided that punishment should not be excessive in comparison to the crime committed. In 1791, Americans, who had recently won independence from the British, sought to perpetuate this type of protection. To that end, the Eighth Amendment was added to the American Bill of Rights. The Eighth Amendment provides that "[e]xcessive bail shall not be required, nor excessive fines imposed, nor cruel and unusual punishments inflicted."

Early on, the Supreme Court did not extend the protections of the Eighth Amendment to state citizens as to punishments inflicted on them by state governments. The amendment was seen as operating only against the federal government. Had that remained the state of the law, the cruel and unusual punishment prohibition in the Constitution would have no impact on the ability of the states to operate chain gangs.

However, the Supreme Court's position with regard to the applicability of the amendment to state action did change. The Court, having previously held that many protections afforded to citizens by the Constitution were only protections against federal action, effectively reversed its position. It did so by extending those protections, which were considered fundamental rights, to state affairs through the Fourteenth Amendment. Thus, "[i]t is now well established that the Eighth Amendment applies to the States through the Fourteenth Amendment." Section One of the Fourteenth Amendment states,

> All persons born or naturalized in the United States, and subject to the jurisdiction thereof, are citizens of the United States and of the State wherein they reside. No State shall make or enforce any law which shall abridge the privileges or immunities of citizens of the United States; nor shall any State deprive any person of life, liberty, or property, without due process of law; nor deny to any person within its jurisdiction the equal protection of the laws.

The Court has used the combined authority it found in the Eighth and Fourteenth Amendments to hold that a particular punishment imposed by a state was unconstitutional. With it settled that there is authority in the United States Constitution which courts may use to put an end to cruel and unusual punishments inflicted by the several states, the analysis turns to whether modern chain gangs fall within the parameters of such impermissible punishment.

WILSON V. KELLY

According to Justice William O. Douglas, the constitutionality of chain gangs "is an important question never decided by the Court." However, there have been decisions which provide substantial direction for such an inquiry. Just four years before Justice Douglas made the above pronouncement in 1972, the Supreme Court, in a per curiam opinion, affirmed a district court case which went a long way toward deciding the issue. In *Wilson v. Kelly*, prisoners in the state of Georgia brought suit to abolish segregation in the Georgia prison system, end employment discrimination in the system, and abolish the work camps maintained by the system. The district court ordered desegregation but found that the prisoners lacked standing to bring the employment discrimination claim. The district court further held that work camps were not "per se" unconstitutional. The court noted that state prisoners are entitled to constitutional protections from state punishment. However, the court held that these protections do not prevent the state from requiring prisoners to engage in hard labor as part of their punishment. The court held that this was true even if those prisoners forced to work are deprived of some rehabilitation programs afforded to other prisoners. The court found that to hold otherwise would be unwise because of the many factors to be considered in determining whether rehabilitation programs are suitable for a particular inmate and because the states have no duty to provide rehabilitation programs to any of their prisoners.

Mike Shelton for the *Orange County Register*. Reprinted by permission.

The principles announced in *Wilson* are bolstered by the Supreme Court's act of affirming the decision and by the holdings of other cases. For instance, in *United States v. Reynolds*, the Supreme Court held that the states undoubtedly have the authority to impose involuntary servitude as punishment for a crime. Additionally, there is said to be a "longstanding policy of the courts not to interfere in prison administration and discipline at any level."

All of this does not necessarily spell doom to any challenge of chain gangs based on Eighth Amendment grounds. The Supreme Court has taken the position that "[t]he [Eighth] Amendment must draw its meaning from the evolving standards of decency that mark the progress of a maturing society." Thus, the door is open for a judicial conclusion that a society as enlightened as ours has no place in it for chain gangs. Furthermore, it has been declared that the states must not jeopardize the safety of their

prisoners. This principle could possibly lead to a successful challenge of chain gangs if it were shown, as some contend, that
chaining men together and having them work in close proximity to roadways constitutes a safety risk. *Wilson* also explicitly left
open the possibility that an inmate could raise a question as to
his particular treatment at a work camp. Moreover, the Eighth
Amendment is said to prohibit "the unnecessary and wanton in-
fliction of pain," according to a trio of Supreme Court justices
in 1976. These principles could provide a conduit for many
challenges to the constitutionality of modern chain gangs.

It is unclear whether a successful constitutional challenge to
chain gangs will materialize. It does seem likely that the use of
prisoners as laborers will not be successfully challenged. After
all, the Thirteenth Amendment on its face recognizes the use of
labor as punishment. Nevertheless, there seems to be room,
through the cracks and holes mentioned above, for a challenge
to chain gangs or at least a particular chain gang as such. However, such a challenge will not easily succeed given the afore-
mentioned precedent. . . .

POLICY CONSIDERATIONS

Setting the constitutional issues aside, there remains an issue as
to whether it is good policy for states to operate chain gangs.
Or, stating the question in perhaps a more answerable form, are
there policy reasons for not operating chain gangs which substantially outweigh the policy considerations which justify their
operation?

Fob James, Alabama's Governor, authored a newspaper article
in which he detailed the policies behind his state's reinstitution
of chain gangs. Governor James stated that Alabama began using
chain gangs again for two reasons. First, some prisoners found
prison life to be so easy that they preferred to remain in jail
rather than be paroled. Second, state officials "felt that medium
risk prisoners should be out working rather than lifting weights
or watching cable TV." Furthermore, Governor James stated that
public safety considerations coupled with personnel concerns
justify the use of chains on these working inmates. For instance,
Governor James contends that one officer can only guard twenty
low-risk prisoners without chains. However, he maintains that
by using chains one officer can watch twice as many prisoners,
as well as more risky prisoners, while imposing less risk upon
the public. Finally, Governor James believes that the use of chain
gangs will deter prisoners from returning to prison.

The sentiments expressed by Governor James are not exclusively propounded by him. Gary Gerbitz, a district attorney in Tennessee, was quoted as stating that the decline in inner city conditions has resulted in some prisoners seeing their quality of life improve when they go to jail. Gerbitz contends that jails are no longer seen by prisoners as punishment. Similarly, Alabama Corrections Commissioner Ron Jones has taken the position that chain gangs will be successful because they will reverse this trend by instilling a fear of prison. Some believe that the chain gangs, when observed at work by the public, will serve to deter others from committing crime.

Crime deterrence and the imposition of fitting punishment are not the only justifications advanced in support of chain gangs. Chain gangs may produce smoother running prisons since chain gang members are so tired after a full day's work that they only want to shower and sleep. It has also been contended that prisoners may actually enjoy having the opportunity to be outside and may thereby find incarceration more tolerable due to the use of chain gangs.

PRISONER ATTITUDES

Perhaps not surprisingly, some prisoners do not agree with the views of chain gang proponents. One inmate, who obviously proves the proponents' point that chain gangs discourage prisoners from returning to prison, demonstrated that his idea of not returning differed somewhat from the deterrent concept behind chain gangs. The inmate was quoted as saying, "[b]efore I come back to the chain gang I'll get on [the television show] 'Most Wanted.'" He also stated that the work he was doing on the chain gang was the "hardest time" he had ever served and that he dreaded the work every day.

Another inmate's comments also provide some insight into the way prisoners feel about chain gangs. In the presence of a newspaper reporter, the inmate who was working on a chain gang busting rocks dabbed some blood from a cut on his wrist onto a rock and said, "[t]ell Jones [the head of the Alabama Department of Corrections] to put his head here."

This sampling of prisoner attitudes may raise questions as to the nature of the impact that chain gang service is having on inmates. Some commentators have concluded that chain gang service will negatively impact inmates and serve no valid purpose. It has been contended that chain gang service will build hatred in inmates. One theory is that chain gangs demean convicts and take away their hope and dignity, thereby producing harder criminals.

Some have questioned the motives behind chain gangs. They note that the public supports chain gangs and thus believe that chain gangs serve only to further the political careers of those who support them.

Still others attack chain gangs on the grounds that prisoners should be doing something else with their time rather than hard chain gang labor. For instance, it is suggested that educating inmates would do more to keep them from returning to crime than does hard labor. It has also been contended that enrolling prisoners in rehabilitation programs would be of greater benefit than chain gangs. Additionally, it has been asserted that prisoners should labor in prison industries to produce revenue for the state rather than busting rocks or cleaning up roads.

No Reason Not to Use Chain Gangs

In short, there are many diverse views concerning whether chain gangs amount to good public policy. The determination is a somewhat subjective one. However, an evaluation of the various views does seem to lead to the conclusion that there is no valid policy reason for the states to refrain from using chain gangs.

First of all, prison is for punishment. This fact is recognized in the Thirteenth Amendment to the United States Constitution which prohibits involuntary servitude "except as punishment for crime." This Amendment also points out the acceptance of forced labor as proper punishment.

As for the argument that prisoners will resent the punishment imposed on chain gangs and thereby become harder criminals, it is hard to take seriously. Should it be policy to ensure that those being punished do not resent their punishment? Should only those punishments which cause the person being punished to feel good be imposed? If this were the case, it seems that the word punishment would have to be redefined.

There does seem to be some merit in the argument that enrolling prisoners in rehabilitation programs would be more likely to stop repeat offenders. In this regard, it is important to note that which was explained in *Wilson*. Namely, many factors impact on whether rehabilitation programs are helpful to a particular inmate. An inmate's past experiences, sentence length, and mental state are all relevant. As the states are in a position to evaluate these factors, there seems to be no compelling reason to take from them the ability to determine which prisoners should or should not be enrolled in rehabilitation programs. This same analysis seems applicable to the argument that convicts should be educated rather than placed on chain gangs. Further, it could be argued that hard work itself is rehabilitative.

The argument that prisoners should work in prison industries that generate income for the state rather than on chain gangs seems to have partial merit. So far as the argument applies to chain gangs that bust rocks, it seems valid. However as it applies to chain gangs which clean roads, it ignores the obvious benefit of clean roadways and the fact that such work by chain gangs may be less competitive with private industry than would other prison labor alternatives.

A Successful Challenge Is Possible

The United States Constitution, for the most part, provides few challenges for states that wish to operate chain gangs. However, it is conceivable that a successful constitutional challenge could be made to chain gangs if the proper facts and the right theory met the right court at the proper time. That is to say that there is precedent which could ripen into trouble for chain gangs, but no clear problem is now present.

As to the policy considerations, there are ample policy concerns to justify the operation of chain gangs which are not substantially countered by contrary views. Thus, policy concerns do not dictate the extinguishment of chain gangs.

In summation, after considering the constitutional and policy concerns, there appears to be no valid reason why states wishing to operate chain gangs as a part of the corrections program should not do so. Perhaps the chain gangs will indeed help state corrections programs to better serve the public. Of course, only time will tell.

| "Most [inmates] will feel anger and hatred at having been physically tortured and humiliated so some politician could grandstand for a short-sighted public."

INMATE CHAIN GANGS ARE AN IMPROPER FORM OF PUNISHMENT

Michael Corsentino

In the following viewpoint, *Prison Life* magazine photographer Michael Corsentino describes his observations of inmate chain gangs from the Limestone Correctional Facility in Alabama. Corsentino argues that authorities use chain gangs as a symbolic measure to gain publicity rather than to achieve any positive results. According to the author, inmates on chain gangs suffer from a variety of physical ailments due to the grueling daylong work and are often abused by their guards. Prisoners who refuse to work on a chain gang are severely disciplined, Corsentino maintains.

As you read, consider the following questions:

1. What privileges are denied to inmates on the Alabama chain gang, according to Corsentino?
2. According to the author, how long do most inmates stay on the chain gang?
3. What is the "Mexican prison," according to Corsentino?

Michael Corsentino, "Back on the Chain Gang," *Prison Life*, November/December 1995. Reprinted by permission of the publisher.

It is the middle of a record heat wave when I arrive at the Limestone Correctional Facility near Huntsville, Alabama. The stone guardtower, set in the center of the prison, casts a long shadow in the blazing afternoon sun. I see the forms of armed guards as they move anonymously behind the tower's tinted windows.

The entrance at Limestone is marked by two brick columns with thick black metal bars between them. I grasp the door handle and look up at the video camera mounted to my left as an unnerving clanging sound cuts through the silence. My arm vibrates and I feel the steel bolt inside the door release. I step through and cross manicured grounds that smell of freshly cut grass—on my way to the administration building.

A tall white man with a thick mustache and easy Southern manner introduces himself as Captain Wise. "Don't take anything from prisoners and don't give anything to prisoners," he says, and radios for a guard to serve as my escort.

A Hot Issue

I am here to photograph prisoners at this medium-security facility. In May 1995, Alabama Governor Fob James Jr. and State Prison Commissioner Ron Jones decided to resurrect the chain gang as part of a much-touted get-tough-on-crime campaign. After having been banned as inhumane punishment for over forty years, the practice of shackling men at the ankles and herding them out to work beside highways has become a hot political issue. The return of the chain gang, which required no state or federal legislation, is seen by critics as a step backward to times when men were treated worse than animals.

In fact, parole violators brought to Limestone have traditionally been assigned to work crews that clear brush along the highway and keep the prison grounds clean. The difference now is that they do the same work chained at the ankles like slaves. The purely symbolic program functions as a means of attracting publicity for politicians and prison officials while humiliating and embittering the prisoners, all of whom are medium-security, nonviolent offenders.

Prisoners who work on the chain gang, 70 percent African American, are housed in separate dorms and denied such privileges as personal visits with family members, educational programs, television, radio, coffee and cigarettes. They are required to spend at least 30 days on the chain gang before they may be redesignated to other work details and living quarters where rudimentary privileges are returned.

I recall movies that portray conditions on a Southern chain

gang. Mervyn LeRoy's classic 1932 film, *I Am a Fugitive from a Chain Gang*, starring Paul Muni, told the story of one man's suffering at the hands of the Georgia chain gang system. When the movie was released, public sentiment was stirred by the brutal treatment prisoners endured. Shortly thereafter, Georgia Governor Ellis Arnall abolished chain gangs and the rest of the nation soon followed suit.

A PRISON TOUR

Five minutes later a guard shows up and motions for the door to be opened. He gives me a tour of the prison facilities, stopping now and then to indicate such points of interest as the inmate-staffed shoe shine room. As we pass, a black prisoner looks up and smiles over a pile of dirty rags and shoe polish canisters. In the infirmary, the guard shows me a room where prisoners with AIDS lie dying. The room is lit only by the blue-gray glow of television screens. Men with gaunt faces eaten away by disease slowly turn and look my way.

The guard tells me the prison has a population of 2,000 men, with 420 assigned to the chain gangs. "No matter what they say," he says, puffing on a short thin cigar, "these people aren't in prison for singing too loudly in church."

Prisoners see the camera equipment and shout to get my attention. "Hey, camera man. You gonna take my picture?"

"Yo, you gonna be my girl?"

The other men laugh.

In Dorm 31, where chain gang prisoners are housed, men eye me as I walk inside the dormitory.

The room is teeming with men. Bunk beds two and three tiers high are jammed together row after row with narrow spaces between them for walkways. An elevated blockhouse used by guards sits in the middle of the open room. More prisoners, just returned from the chain gang, start making their way inside. My escort leaves me and mounts the blockhouse.

After a strip search, the men troop into an open, tiled room for showering. Nearby, others sit on exposed toilets. The smell of 400 men hangs in stagnant air; a large ceiling fan does little more than push around the stench and humidity.

INMATE EXPERIENCES

One prisoner lies on a top bunk reading a worn edition of *The Fugitive*; the man below him is already fast asleep, his feet dangling off the end of the bed. The prisoners are anxious to share their experiences, to tell me stories about the chain gang. They want people to know how they feel. Many violated parole simply by giving a dirty urine sample. I ask a few how long they've been on the chain gang, and they shout the number of days:

"Eighty-three."

"One hundred and eleven."

"Ninety-eight."

They explain that automatic disciplinary extensions handed out for infractions make it rare for anyone to leave after only 30 days. The usual stay is from three to six months or longer. An orientation sheet for newcomers lists reasons for extension: showing up late for work, not being properly shaved, not having your bed made to the satisfaction of the shift guard or disrespecting an officer. Extensions range from three to six months on top of time already served, and a prisoner with a bad attitude can end up on the chain gang indefinitely.

DISCRIMINATORY AND DEGRADING

Chain gangs make a great photo opportunity for vote-conscious politicians. However, those who support them tend to overlook two points. First, for many, chain gangs are a painful reminder of the injustices of the postbellum South. Although Alabama touts its chain gangs as modern and integrated, many cannot forget that, historically, chain gangs were developed as punishment for ex-slaves and their descendants who committed crimes. In the early 1900s, twice as many blacks than whites were on chain gangs. And today in Alabama prisons, where chain gangs are operated only in the disciplinary segregation unit, it is not unusual for the chain gang to be 90 percent African American.

Second, and just as important, intentionally degrading and humiliating inmates not only makes for bad corrections policy, it violates the Eighth Amendment to the Constitution. After all, as the U.S. Supreme Court has recognized: "The basic concept underlying the Eighth Amendment is nothing less than the dignity of man."

Rhonda Brownstein, *Corrections Today*, April 1996.

A few convicts show me their bodies, parts of which are covered with severe outbreaks of poison ivy and other skin diseases from working on the chain gang. One man pulls up his shirt and lowers his pants to reveal scabbed red skin covering most of his body, the result of infestation by chiggers—parasitic, bloodsucking mites that burrow under the skin and cause intense irritation. Another man displays his swollen red feet, raw with large, fluid-filled blisters.

An overhead speaker crackles a garbled announcement. The guards take a head count. Lining up single file, the men enter the dining hall and shuffle along the cafeteria line while servers fill their trays. Meatloaf of soy and gristle is tonight's fare.

Between bites, men speak of rising tension in the prison. If things don't change, they say, a riot will break out. With another 200 beds soon to be added, all bunks will be three beds high, bringing the number of men in the already overcrowded dorm to 630. Just the day before, 20 shanks were found in the unit. Still hungry, the men I sit with ask for the leftovers from my plate.

A CHAIN GANG AT WORK

The next morning at six, prisoners are checked out for the day. After being patted down, they board buses one by one, followed by drivers lugging milk crates full of leg irons. The lead bus pulls out, trailed by a convoy of five others, along with several vans and station wagons. After a 20-minute drive, the buses stop in staggered formation along route I-65.

Prisoners exit the buses slowly and stand waiting. Guards order them onto all fours. Working in two-man teams, guards shackle prisoners together in groups of five. Many men wear two pairs of socks to avoid skin burns caused by leg irons rubbing against their flesh. The chain gang workers pick up rakes, garden shears and bow saws from an open trailer.

The long work day beams. The men spend hours hobbling around, tripping over the chains and each other as they remove trees and clear brush, clean up litter and pull weeds. As cars and semis speed by, drivers honk, yell and howl at the chain gang prisoners.

Guards sitting by the roadside shout an occasional order. Each guard has his own group of prisoners to watch and his own style of supervision. A young guard, chewing a wooden match stick, explains his philosophy: "These kind of people just aren't constituted for work. We get 'em out here and show 'em how to work. This way when they leave, they won't wanna come back. They'll know what work is." He adjusts the shotgun over his shoulder and continues. "The thing is, we're keeping 'em safe. Without the chains they'd try to escape, and we'd have to shoot 'em."

Farther north on the interstate, a bored guard tells the men in his crew that he is dissatisfied with the job they're doing; he explains they are not responding quickly enough to his orders. He pulls a wing-nut from his pocket, fixes on a location and throws the nut into the weeds and grass. He yells to his group to come forward. They shuffle over and he indicates the general direction of the wing-nut, then orders them to get on their hands and knees and search until they find it. This diversion lasts two hours.

The first break, five hours after work began, is for lunch. Prisoners complain about meager portions. One man holds a sandwich made of a single piece of crusty processed cheese between slices of dry white bread. In disgust, he throws the stiff piece of cheese on the ground.

"Real cheese would melt," he says.

INMATE HUMILIATION

Chain gang prisoners from the disciplinary lock-up unit have it worse. The first to leave their cells in the morning and the last to return at the end of the day, they swing hatchets and pickaxes for ten hours. Chained in fives, they tug, pull and hack at tree stumps. The chains make already difficult work hellish.

After laboring all day in the sweltering heat, men on the stump-digging detail begin walking the six miles back to the prison. They stop at the Limestone Facility farm to cool off and get a drink of water.

"The worst thing is the humiliation of being chained to other men," a prisoner named Gooden tells me. "The state has made me their slave. I'm not a man anymore."

Men chained to him listen and nod. "We were doing the same work as before, only now they chain us up like animals so the governor can make it look like he's doing something about crime. All this shit is doing is making people angry. When we get out, we're not going to be in a good mood."

The guards have their own story. "On my chain gang," says one, "I try to be as fair as possible, not like some others. I mean, if it's really hot, I'll work my guys in the shade if they're getting tired." He lifts his hat and wipes the sweat from his brow. "If two guys want to beat the shit out of each other, that's okay, too. As long as they don't fight with tools, I figure let them settle their disputes like men. Now if they pick up tools, that's a different story. Then I have to fire on them. If they try anything, I have to put them down. Buckshot spreads out, I might take out more than one. I don't ask questions, though. My main objective is to stop what's going on and regain control. They pretty much stay in line."

The guard smirks and says what I've heard at least five times in the last two days: "You know, they ain't in here for singing too loudly in church."

"Right," says another guard. "That's right."

Prisoners ask if I've photographed the "Mexican prison" or

the "hitching post." The hitching post resembles the kind of post used to hitch a horse, only this one is built for men who refuse to work on the chain gang. Stubborn convicts are hand-cuffed and chained to the post at four in the morning and un-chained 12 hours later. Because the post is not tall enough to al-low a man to stand straight, nor short enough to allow him to sit, being chained to the post forces the prisoner to bend over all day in the Alabama sun.

The Mexican prison is an outdoor cage with barbed wire strung along the top. The floor, embedded with jagged rocks, makes it uncomfortable, if not impossible, for prisoners to sit or lie down. Locked in the pen for 12 hours, the men stand in the sun and wait. "It's called the Mexican prison because inmates locked inside bake in the sun all day," a prisoner explains and kicks the ground, causing a cloud of dust to rise.

OFFICIALS' PERSPECTIVE

On my last day at Limestone I meet Acting Warden Ralph Hooks, a reserved man who sits placidly behind a large wooden desk when I am shown into his office. I notice there are no family photographs on his desk. He has neatly arranged piles of paper-work spread before him. In well-rehearsed sound bites, Hooks explains the benefits of the chain-gang program. He stresses its cost-effectiveness, and quickly points out that leg irons provide a safe work environment for prisoners. "They also build charac-ter," Hooks asserts.

I mention what the men told me, that they had been doing the same work more effectively before the cumbersome leg irons were introduced.

"It's a matter of budget," Hooks continues, dropping his ar-gument for character development. Where once it required two armed guards to watch over a detail, the leg irons make it possi-ble for one guard to supervise 40 chained prisoners.

The prison had to lay out an initial cost of over $17,000 for the leg irons. But chaining convicts allowed prison administra-tors to reduce the guard staff and cut payroll. The practice has also enabled the governor and prison commissioner to turn Limestone into a media sideshow while winning points with vengeful voters. The real cost of the chain gangs, however, is still unknown.

Two days after I left Alabama, Prison Commissioner Ron Jones, basking in a spotlight of media attention, announced an-other innovative work detail. Men on the chain gang will spend their days breaking large boulders into small rocks with sledgehammers and pickaxes. Neither the prison nor the state highway department has any need for the crushed rock. As the work can be done more efficiently by a machine, with no guards required, one can only surmise that this is another program designed to build character.

Politicians who champion the use of chain gangs as a deterrent to recidivism may be more concerned with public perception than with social reality. For when they are released, men from the Alabama chain gang will know little more than how to pull weeds, dig stumps and break rocks. Along with these job skills, they will be given $10 and a bus ticket. Most will feel anger and hatred at having been physically tortured and humiliated so some politician could grandstand for a short-sighted public.

As to what kind of character the chain gangs build, America has seen the damage this degrading and futile form of punishment did to the national character decades ago and rejected it as evil.

PERIODICAL BIBLIOGRAPHY

The following articles have been selected to supplement the diverse views presented in this chapter. Addresses are provided for periodicals not indexed in the *Readers' Guide to Periodical Literature*, the *Alternative Press Index*, the *Social Sciences Index*, or the *Index to Legal Periodicals and Books*.

Vince Beiser — "Look for the Prison Label," *Village Voice*, May 21, 1996.

Rhonda Brownstein — "Chain Gangs Are Cruel and Unusual Punishment," *Corrections Today*, April 1996.

Charlie Crist — "Chain Gangs Are Right for Florida," *Corrections Today*, April 1996.

Mark Dunmire — "Inside Jobs: Legalized U.S. Prison Sweatshops Can Cost You Your Job," *People's Weekly World*, February 3, 1996. Available from 235 W. 23rd St., New York, NY 10011.

Larry S. Fischer and Robert Martone — "Putting Intermittent Prisoners to Work," *American Jails*, March/April 1996. Available from American Jail Association, 2053 Day Rd., Suite 100, Hagerstown, MD 21740-9795.

Susan G. Hauser — "Look for the Prison Label," *Wall Street Journal*, April 21, 1995.

Lucia Hwang — "Working for Nothing," *Third Force*, July/August 1996.

Bechetta A. Jackson — "Is the Alabama Prison System's Return to the Chain Gang Unfair to Blacks?" *Jet*, September 18, 1995.

Christian Parenti — "Making Prison Pay," *Nation*, January 29, 1996.

Andrew Peyton Thomas — "Jailhouse Work," *Weekly Standard*, March 4, 1996. Available from News America Publishing, 1211 Ave. of the Americas, New York, NY 10036.

John L. Zalusky — "Convicts in the Workplace? It Makes Them Slaves," *World & I*, March 1996. Available from 3600 New York Ave. NE, Washington, DC 20002.

CHAPTER 4

WHAT ARE THE ALTERNATIVES TO PRISONS?

CHAPTER PREFACE

In May 1995, a California judge sentenced Bob, a consultant who had failed to provide child support, to one year of home confinement with an electronic surveillance anklet. Bob, one of tens of thousands of Americans ordered to wear an electronic monitor, called the device "terrific" because it enabled him to avoid imprisonment and continue his business from his home.

Many criminal justice experts contend that electronic monitoring is a sensible alternative to incarcerating first-time or nonviolent offenders. This option, they argue, frees jail and prison space for more hardened criminals and costs much less than incarceration. In many cases, supporters note, the offenders themselves help pay the daily cost of operating the tracking bracelet. According to defense lawyer John W. Barton, "It's an absolutely wonderful procedure. It saves us as taxpayers tens and tens of thousands of dollars. And it's a punishment."

But detractors assert that electronic monitoring is merely a symbolic punishment and has many flaws. They cite, for example, a U.S. Department of Justice study that concludes that the use of such devices does not save money or make more cell space available. Most importantly, opponents contend, monitoring devices do not deter many offenders from committing other crimes. They point out that, in recent years, suspects in Chicago, Los Angeles, Oakland, and other cities have been charged with committing murder while wearing electronic cuffs. Critics further maintain that offenders who violate the terms of home confinement may go undetected because of technical or human error.

Technological advances may expand the electronic monitoring of offenders—including such innovations as the monitoring of participants' vital signs for possible drug abuse and the discharge of electronic shocks—but may also ignite further controversy. The viewpoints in the following chapter examine the debate around monitoring and other alternatives to prison.

| "An expanded range of sentencing options gives judges greater latitude to exercise discretion in selecting punishments."

ALTERNATIVE SENTENCING CAN SUCCEED

William M. DiMascio

Alternative sentencing includes options such as community service, financial restitution, halfway houses, and intensive supervision probation for nonviolent offenders. In the following viewpoint, excerpted from a report commissioned by the philanthropic Edna McConnell Clark Foundation, William M. DiMascio asserts that intermediate sanctions are less restrictive and less costly than incarceration and can help reduce prison overcrowding and promote rehabilitation. DiMascio, a communications consultant in Villanova, Pennsylvania, contends that alternative sentencing gives judges greater latitude in selecting punishments that more closely fit offenders' crimes.

As you read, consider the following questions:

1. What did an evaluation of Florida's intensive supervision probation program show, according to DiMascio?
2. According to the author, what form of punishment do many European countries use more than the United States?
3. What are some of the community-service activities performed by offenders, according to DiMascio?

Excerpted from William M. DiMascio, "Seeking Justice: Crime and Punishment in America," published by the Edna McConnell Clark Foundation, New York, N.Y., 1995. Reprinted by permission of the publisher.

I ncreasingly, advocates for more effective sentencing practices are calling for a range or continuum of punishment options that provides graduated levels of supervision and harshness. Simple probation is at one end, traditional incarceration at the other, and a variety of community-based sanctions, such as work release, electronic monitoring and community service, bridge the middle ground.

Using a sentencing scheme of this sort enables authorities to maintain expensive prison cells to incapacitate violent criminals. At the same time, less restrictive community-based treatment programs and restitution-focused sentences punish nonviolent offenders, while teaching them accountability for their actions and heightening their chances for rehabilitation. An expanded range of sentencing options gives judges greater latitude to exercise discretion in selecting punishments that more closely fit the circumstances of the crime and the offender. The approach treats prisons as the backstop, rather than the backbone, of the corrections system.

APPLYING INTERMEDIATE SANCTIONS

Intermediate sanctions are most often used for offenders who are considered nonviolent and low-risk. Such punishments usually require the offender to lead a productive life in the community by finding work, doing unpaid community service, learning new skills, paying restitution to victims, enrolling in a treatment or educational program—or all of the above.

Although 25 states have passed community corrections laws and many others have created various kinds of intermediate sanctions between probation and prison, such punishments are not yet being used for a large number of offenders in the United States.

According to a national census conducted by the Bureau of Justice Statistics, there were 698,570 inmates housed in state and federal confinement facilities in 1990, yet only 17,079 offenders serving their sentence in community-based facilities that regularly permit offenders to leave the premises on work or study release, or to participate in other outside programs.

COSTS OF INTERMEDIATE PUNISHMENTS

Annual costs for the various sanctions available within the continuum of intermediate punishments vary from county to county and state to state. In virtually all cases, the cost of alternative sanctions is lower than incarceration.

A 1994 survey of programs in Colorado, North Carolina,

Ohio and Virginia found the following average annual costs of operations (exclusive of capital construction) per participant in these states: probation, $869; intensive supervision, $2,292; community service, $2,759; day reporting, $2,781; house arrest, $402; electronic monitoring, $2,011; halfway house, $12,494; boot camp, $23,707; jail, $14,363, and prison, $17,794.

Boot camps combine the cost of incarceration with additional services such as education, job readiness skills, drug treatment and others. When economies are realized, they usually result from the shortened length of stay in boot camps—on average six months or less. . . .

The administrative structure of alternative sanctions is at the discretion of the local government or courts and sometimes varies considerably among different jurisdictions. The programs can be operated, for example, by the probation departments or by private agencies which report to the courts.

The number of programs and their official titles also vary widely depending on the needs and resources of the local government. Most programs enact harsh consequences for non-compliance with the terms of the sentence, sometimes including jail or prison sentences.

The following section provides a descriptive, although not exhaustive, list of available sanctions. . . .

INTENSIVE SUPERVISION PROBATION (ISP)

This sanction allows offenders to live at home, but under relatively severe restrictions. Offenders in ISP programs usually are required to perform community service, attend school or treatment programs, work, meet with a probation officer (or team of two officers) as often as five times a week, and submit to curfews, employment checks and tests for drug and alcohol use. . . .

By 1990, one or more jurisdictions in every state had implemented ISP programs, primarily for property offenders, yet the effectiveness and the cost savings from the programs have varied widely depending on how they have been structured and administered. Early evaluations of an ISP program operated by the Georgia Department of Corrections concluded that the program had both lowered recidivism rates and prison admissions. But a study of 14 jurisdictions across the country, sponsored by the Department of Justice and conducted by RAND [a California research corporation], indicated that ISP on average had not reduced the total cost of correctional services, in part because the offenders targeted for participation would not have drawn significant prison time. The study also showed that the programs generally did not reduce recidivism, but that recidivism among ISP participants was more often related to technical violations of the demanding conditions of intensive probation than to new crimes. And those technical violations were more often caught because of the increased supervision.

Other evaluations have shown that some carefully designed and managed intensive supervision programs yield better-than-average results. In Florida, for example, corrections officials found that they could spend a fraction of what it costs to send an offender to prison by imposing a community penalty instead. An evaluation of their ISP program, called the Florida Community Control Program (FCCP), concluded that graduates commit new crimes at a lower rate than a comparable group of offenders released from prison.

This study, by the National Council on Crime and Delinquency, further revealed that FCCP saved the state $2,750 per offender, even after hidden costs of intensive supervision were taken into account. The first of these hidden costs is the financial burden of sanctions—usually prison or jail time—imposed on participants who violate the conditions of the program. The second is the cost of "widening the net"—providing a higher, more expensive level of supervision for offenders who probably would have been sentenced to regular probation.

The study's estimate of the financial benefits of FCCP is conservative: researchers did not take into account the supervision fees paid by the offenders in the program or the victim restitution, taxes and child support paid because the offenders were able to hold down a job while participating in the program.

Together, these studies suggest that reaping the full benefits of ISP requires careful targeting to assure that a substantial number of participants would have received appreciable prison time and the use of a range of responses to technical violations so as to limit the use of incarceration when violations occur.

RESTITUTION AND FINES

Monetary penalties involve either restitution, which requires the offender to compensate his or her victim; or fines, in which a set amount is paid to the courts; or both. Usually, the amount is based on the crime and, in some jurisdictions, also on the offender's ability to pay. Restitution is paid to the victim either directly or through state and federal victim compensation funds. The aim of this penalty is to compensate victims for their losses, while teaching offenders financial responsibility. Restitution and fines are sometimes coupled with another penalty, such as probation, community service or treatment.

Day Fines. Many European countries use fines more frequently than the United States, often as the sole punishment for specific crimes. Germany, for example, has used day fines—in which the amount of the fine is determined according to the offender's daily income—as a penalty for as many as 82 percent of adult offenders.

In essence, day fines attempt to equalize the financial impact of the sentence on the offender, addressing the concern that fines are unduly harsh on poor offenders and permit affluent offenders easily to buy their way out of more punitive sanctions.

HUMANE TREATMENT FOR OFFENDERS

[The National Center for Institutions and Alternatives has proposed] a wide range of things: community service; restitution to the victim; if necessary, various forms of supervision within the community; drug or alcohol treatment programs. We try to do for the average offender what a thinking, compassionate, middle-class parent or brother or son would do for someone in their family were they in trouble—that is, design some kind of program that would hopefully prevent the person from committing any more crimes, but also that would try to deal with that person decently and humanely. And we try, as much as possible, to divert them from the criminal-justice system, and certainly from the correctional system, which we see as ultimately much more destructive than helpful.

Jerome Miller, *Humanist*, January/February 1994.

The Vera Institute of Justice has been developing the day fine concept in this country. Judges in Phoenix now use FARE (Financial Assessment Related to Employability) Probation, a form of a day fine, as an alternative to traditional probation in felony cases involving low-risk offenders. Under a FARE Probation sentence, a certain number of units are assigned to a particular offense on the basis of its seriousness—30 units for credit card forgery, for example, or 160 units for a burglary. Each unit is then transferred into a dollar amount based on the offender's income. The penalty amounts have ranged from $180 for a laborer with six children convicted of making a false statement in an unemployment claim to a $22,000 fine for a restaurant owner convicted of money-laundering.

Victim-Offender Mediation. Restitution is sometimes coupled with victim-offender mediation programs, which have emerged in the past two decades across the United States and Europe. These programs allow victims to meet face to face with the offender in the presence of a trained mediator to negotiate a fair restitution agreement. A 1992 study, conducted by the Minnesota Citizens Council on Crime and Justice in cooperation with the University of Minnesota, reported that approximately 100 such programs exist in the United States. Surveying programs in Albuquerque, Austin, Minneapolis, St. Paul and San Francisco, researchers found that 79 percent of the victims and 87 percent of the offenders who participate expressed satisfaction with the results of the mediation process. The restitution was paid in full in 81 percent of the mediated cases, compared to 58 percent of the cases ordered by the courts without mediation. Furthermore, victims generally noted a significant reduction of personal anxiety and fear.

COMMUNITY SERVICE

Community service can be used alone or with other penalties and services, including treatment for substance abuse, restitution or probation. Offenders in community service programs are usually assigned to work for government or private non-profit agencies; they paint churches, maintain parks, collect roadside trash and renovate schools and nursing homes.

Community service programs began in 1966 in Alameda County, California, when municipal court judges decided to sentence certain traffic offenders to periods of unpaid labor. By the late 1980s, some form of community service sanction was in use in all 50 states. The Bureau of Justice Statistics estimates conservatively that 6 percent of all felons nationally are sentenced to perform community service, often in conjunction with other sanctions. Washington State has probably made the most extensive use of the concept: one-third of its convicted felons receive sentences that involve community service.

The Vera Institute of Justice in New York City developed one of the best-monitored and evaluated community service programs in the country. Its Community Service Sentencing Project, now run by the Center for Alternative Sentencing and Employment Services (CASES), works with offenders convicted of misdemeanors who would otherwise receive jail sentences ranging from 15 days to six months. Over a two-week period, offenders perform 70 hours of supervised community service. Since the program began in 1979, approximately 18,000 offenders have participated. In fiscal year 1994, 1,809 offenders were sentenced to the program with a completion rate of 65 percent. Those who do not complete the program are resentenced following a report from CASES. . . .

NONPRISON RESIDENTIAL PROGRAMS

Many states have experimented with residential programs, designed to put offenders in structured settings, such as halfway houses, which allow them to leave the premises for work or other approved activities like drug treatment.

One residential model that has been widely adopted throughout the country is the restitution center. First developed in Wisconsin and Minnesota, restitution centers control and provide support for residents, who must pay victim restitution and child support out of earnings from working in the community.

The Griffin Diversion Center, established in the early 1970s in Griffin, Georgia, earned high praise from the community, in part because the director and staff aggressively built relationships with judges and the local business community. "Work, education and community are the foundation of this program," says the former director of the Center, James Fletcher.

Residents work eight hours a day, take care of all the Center's maintenance, perform community service on weekends, attend classes or counseling sessions in the evening and submit to regular drug testing. They also participate in sports tournaments and organize food and clothing drives. Residents are considered valuable workers by area businesses, and the program has faced virtually no resistance from its neighbors. . . .

THE VALUE OF INTERMEDIATE SANCTIONS

The unprecedented growth in the nation's prison population has placed a heavy economic burden on taxpayers, in terms of both the fiscal cost of building, maintaining and operating prisons and jails and the human cost of an offender's lost potential and the destabilized families that are left behind. In addition, overcrowded prisons are hard to manage and invite disorder and even riot. Intermediate sanctions are a valuable resource to lessen these problems. Moreover, they provide a means for offenders who are not dangerous to repay their victims and their communities. Intermediate sanctions also promote rehabilitation—which most citizens want, but most prisons are no longer able to provide—and the reintegration of the offender into the community. And once the programs are in place, they do this at a comparatively low cost.

High quality sanctions must be thoughtfully conceived, effectively targeted, well-planned and well-staffed. Although they can be less expensive than prison, they should not be done cheaply. The task has the added complexities of controlling behavior in the less restrictive setting of the community.

Incarceration is appropriate for offenders who endanger the community. Finding the space to incarcerate them, however, can be problematic, since prisons have been filled with offenders for whom intermediate sanctions may provide a reasonable and effective form of punishment. Increasingly, even in a period of inflamed public opinion about crime, citizens are embracing the concept of punishments without prisons for nonviolent offenders. This approach saves prison resources for violent and career offenders.

| *"Alternative programs have actually increased the total number of offenders in the [prison] system."*

ALTERNATIVE SENTENCING HAS NOT SUCCEEDED

Corey Pearson

In the following viewpoint, Corey Pearson argues that alternative sentences have failed to significantly reduce recidivism or prison overcrowding. He contends that alternative sentences are largely given to middle-class offenders whose income has enabled them to avoid imprisonment, while poor offenders are sentenced to prison. Pearson contends that by creating dual systems—prison for lower-class offenders and alternative sentencing for the more affluent—"society is doing nothing for most prisoners." Pearson is a former volunteer with the Prisoners' Rights Union in Sacramento, California.

As you read, consider the following questions:

1. What is the most commonly touted benefit of incarceration, according to Pearson?
2. According to Pearson, what method do some criminals use to apologize for their crimes?
3. In the author's opinion, how do budget cuts impact alternative programs?

Corey Pearson, "Alternative Sentencing," *California Prisoner*, Winter 1992. Reprinted by permission of the Prisoners' Rights Union, Sacramento, California.

Criminal justice has taken a sharp turn to the right in the last few decades. Citizens regularly contact their legislators seeking mandatory sentences, longer prison sentences, reactivation of the death penalty, and laws that will send juveniles to prisons with adult prisoners. It is common practice for California's legislators to sit together and add offenses to the already long list calling for mandatory sanctions, such as longer sentences—all the result of society's demands for "get tough" measures.

The violence of contemporary corrections has a way of feeding on itself, creating more of the same, so it is likely that sooner rather than later we will be immersed in an unproductive morass, an even more costly prison system that does little to lessen crime in our streets. Then it is probable that the pendulum will swing back and rehabilitation of offenders will be the demand, with the public naively believing that outmoded approaches will do the trick and decrease crime.

THE COSTS OF PRISON

If a balance sheet was presented on the cost-benefit of locking up offenders as a solution to the crime problem, the tally would shock most of the public and might even discourage the practice. It presently costs an average of $15,000 to lock up one person for one year in this country. In many states, the cost is as high as $35,000. In addition, it costs over $70,000 just to build one new prison cell. At these prices, an offender could be sent to one of the better colleges each year and have plenty of spending money left over.

And what are the benefits of locking up these offenders? The one we hear the most is incapacitation: at least the offender will not be on the streets committing crime. But at what total expense?

Prisons certainly incapacitate for as long as the person is incarcerated. However, recent studies have shown that even incapacitation of habitual criminals will minimally affect overall crime rates, so society is incurring substantial costs with negligible benefits.

Liberals have pressed for rehabilitation, but their approaches to reform have not been innovative enough. They have sometimes advocated bringing professionals into the prison. Psychiatrists, social workers, sociologists, and psychologists have set up shop there with their tools of treatment, training, and diagnosis (i.e., transactional analysis, positive peer culture, and psychotherapy). Unfortunately, it has not worked. Generally, treatment in prison is known for its failure.

Another proposed reform is to get offenders out of institutions, through alternative programs like halfway houses, work-release, probation, and electronic house arrest of the offender. Middle-class offenders have already benefitted from fairly restrictive work-release programs and halfway houses as well as the more permissive options of weekends in jail, community supervision, public service stints, and restitution schemes.

Work-release programs are commonly used in American corrections, and the public is probably more familiar with this alternative than any of the others. Offenders on work-release reside at an institution or halfway house but are released during the day to work at a noninstitutional job.

DESERVED IMPRISONMENT

Anti-prison advocates have found "selective incapacitation" to be a wonderfully elastic concept. In the name of incarcerating only the most serious offenders, they have narrowly redefined what a "serious" offender is. Today, virtually all property criminals, child molesters, and even many violent offenders are being described as "minor" or "low-risk" offenders. These, advocates assert, should not be in prison at all, but instead be allowed "alternatives to incarceration" that would keep them out in the community.

However, we are already using such "community alternatives" to the hilt. Today, three-quarters of all convicted criminals are free either on probation or parole. And notwithstanding deceptive claims to the contrary, the overwhelming majority of state prison inmates deserve to be there. Ninety-four percent of state inmates have been convicted either of a violent crime, or have past criminal convictions.

Robert James Bidinotto, *Law Enforcement Alliance of America Advocate*, Summer/Fall 1995.

The rules and characteristics vary from state to state; in some states an offender must find a job himself before he will be admitted to a program, but in other states a job is provided to an offender who is deemed worthy of the program. Wages vary, again, from state to state. Often if an offender earns a decent wage, he must pay a percentage back to the state Department of Corrections; this can be anywhere from 30 to 90 percent and, ironically, amounts to an offender paying to stay incarcerated, since the state considers its percentage as payment for room and board.

If an offender is lucky, his prison sentence will also be shortened by serving the end of his time within a halfway house. Here he lives with four to one hundred other residents in a less restrictive setting, and may work in the surrounding community. Halfway houses provide supervision for an offender trying to readjust to life in the community. It is possible that an offender could be sent to a halfway house in lieu of a prison stay, but this sentencing option is rarely used.

Also rarely used are programs known as study-release, whereby offenders attend colleges or universities instead of working in the community.

Since halfway houses are located within the community, offenders with violent histories are usually not granted residence in them, as is also true of work-release and study-release participation. Drug and psychiatric halfway houses, however, are more likely to admit problem offenders since their rules are very restrictive.

Generally, for the first third of their stay, offenders are not allowed any visits to the community, but furloughs become more frequent as the offender undergoes more treatment. This approach to rehabilitation works best when the setting closely resembles a family, with staff showing a genuine concern for individual offenders and allowing them to develop self-esteem and personal values.

Splitting Time

Less restrictive, and much more innovative, is the weekends-in-jail option. An offender sentenced in this way spends from Friday night or Saturday morning to Sunday night or Monday morning locked up, but during the rest of the week he is a community resident. The idea is that he should be punished by having some of his liberties withheld, but that completely pulling him out of his home would be unnecessary.

Often this alternative is used in combination with another, public service work. The sentence calls for weekends or evenings spent volunteering at an agency or public service organization. Offenders have spent time working in nursing homes, boys' clubs, counseling agencies, and a number of other settings. This option is usually reserved for misdemeanants.

The courts have also started using community supervision; offenders, in addition to having a probation officer, are placed with a third-party advocate who helps them stay on the right track. These advocates may, for example, help an offender find a job, child care, or counseling. Advocates are provided by offender assistance organizations.

One alternative that has received some attention is financial restitution. An offender who is able to pay back his victim does so. Unfortunately, in the past, many offenders did not have the means to participate in this kind of plan. Currently, courts are starting to recognize the usefulness of payment schedules. Both offenders and victims can benefit when the courts allow an offender to pay his victim back on a supervised schedule.

MONITORING OFFENDERS

In September 1986, a suburban community near New York City began testing with electronic house arrest devices. Probationers selected for the program were required to be housebound when not at work. To make sure they complied, each person wore a futuristic ball and chain: a 4-oz. radio transmitter that was attached to the ankle with tamperproof plastic straps. If the wearer strayed more than one hundred feet from his home, a computer would have flashed a note for the probation officer.

This program has since been enhanced by the use of television monitoring within the home for each participant, and telephone relays to ensure that the person is where he or she belongs at random times during the day and/or night. The initial tests for the anklets were done in New Mexico in 1983, and much progress has continued since that time.

One of the latest alternatives to imprisonment is requiring criminals to apologize for crimes committed in an advertisement in the local newspaper. The apologies advertised begin with a history of prior criminal activity and an explanation of the most recent crime committed by the offender. It then follows with the apology from the offender.

The ads are paid for by the criminals. In the past, all of the criminals were repeat offenders and chose to place the advertisement rather than serve time in prison. What makes this program even better, from the viewpoint of the state, is that it costs the state nothing.

What helps an alternative to work, lowering recidivism, enabling offenders to function more productively, and ultimately affecting the level of violence which sustains the culture of crime? One factor is the presence of an advocate who works with the offender at least thirty hours a week, or whenever the offender is tempted—a paid or volunteer support system. The fundamental concern is that the programs demonstrate both care and supervision for the individual. However, because these programs focus on the individual's needs, they do not replicate easily.

Do Alternatives Work?

So are alternatives more successful? Are they more cost effective?

The answer to these questions is mixed. The primary problem with alternatives is that they generally have not been tried for the population that would otherwise be in prison. The programs which work are usually reserved for populations which have the means to avoid falling into the criminal justice system abyss—generally the middle class.

"Money talks and bullshit walks," as the saying goes, echoed by blacks, hispanics, and the poor within the jails of America. Thus, those with money will be heard, and either go free or go into a select alternative program. Those without money and/or resources walk, generally, in one direction—towards incarceration in one of the already overcrowded and dismal prisons.

In practice that means that alternative programs have actually increased the total number of offenders in the system. By creating dual systems, with prison for the lower class criminals, and alternatives for those who rarely go to prison, society is doing nothing for most prisoners.

In order for the system to change, someone has to admit that the system needs to change. Authentic alternatives have been given little opportunity to succeed. The typical state corrections department allocates 95 percent of its funds for the prisons.

Because of a tradition of dealing with light-weight offenders unlikely to be incarcerated anyway, alternatives are considered luxuries rather than necessities, superfluous rather than required. When budget cuts become necessary, alternatives are the first to go. Had they been true alternatives to prison, reflected in lower numbers of imprisoned inmates, this probably would not be the pattern.

"Intensive probation is one of the
most underutilized alternatives to
incarceration."

PAROLE AND PROBATION CAN
SUCCEED AS ALTERNATIVES

National Criminal Justice Commission

In the following viewpoint, the National Criminal Justice Commission argues that parole and probation are valid sentencing alternatives that can succeed when they are well implemented.
The commission contends that these alternatives require adequate resources to succeed and that the role of parole and probation officers should be to help offenders find jobs, overcome
drug problems, and become more responsible citizens. Intensive
probation—which involves multiple contacts per week between
probation officers and offenders—costs less than incarceration
and should be considered as a sentencing option, the commission maintains. The National Criminal Justice Commission was
formed in 1994 by the National Center on Institutions and Alternatives to study and make recommendations concerning
American criminal justice policy.

As you read, consider the following questions:

1. How did the role of probation systems change in the 1980s,
   according to the commission?
2. What do the authors mean by "intensive probation"?
3. What criticism does the commission have of California's
   parole policy?

Excerpts from The Real War on Crime: The Report of the National Criminal Justice Commission, Steven
R. Donziger, ed. Copyright ©1996 by the National Center on Institutions and
Alternatives. Reprinted by permission of HarperPerennial, a division of HarperCollins
Publishers, Inc.

The roots of probation in America reach to 1841, when John Augustus, a shoemaker, visited Boston's criminal court. As a judge was about to send a drunk off to jail, Augustus intervened and offered to look after the man. Three weeks later, Augustus returned to court. The man he had taken was sober and remorseful. The Court soon gave Augustus other cases, and by 1878, Boston had instituted the nation's first full-fledged probation system for adults.

Probation today is the most commonly used sanction in the criminal justice system. In 1994, two-thirds of all people under criminal justice supervision, or about three million people, were on probation. Most of the people on probation committed crimes of the lowest measurable severity—driving with a suspended license, petty larceny, and possession of small amounts of controlled substances.

Offenders who are put on probation are released to the community under the supervision of a probation officer. The supervision often consists of nothing but brief weekly or monthly meetings. Probation is usually combined with a series of orders that require the offender to stay away from a certain person or place, to abstain from using drugs or drinking alcohol, and to seek and hold a job. The average cost of probation is about $850 per offender per year. In many states, probationers are required to contribute earnings toward the cost of supervision.

Few people believe the probationary system is successful in helping to reduce crime in America. This is not surprising in light of the fundamental strife in the goals and priorities of probationary sentences. In the 1960s and 1970s, probation officers believed that their mission was to rehabilitate offenders, whom they regarded as clients. The goal was to increase community safety by supervising offenders closely and helping them adjust to community life. Probation officers helped their clients to find work, overcome drug problems, and maintain family and community responsibility. In the 1980s, probation systems reacted to the harsher political climate and recast their role in terms of punishment. They focused on catching offenders for violations and largely abandoned efforts to help the offender solve the problems that may have led to the offense.

HUGE CASELOADS

Like other parts of the system, most probation programs are bogged down with huge caseloads. While a caseload of approximately 30 probationers is considered optimal, most probation officers carry caseloads of 200 and higher. The volume alone prevents most probation officers from getting actively involved with offenders in an individualized manner, either in a support-ive or punitive capacity. Offenders who commit income tax eva-sion and those who commit armed robbery require different strategies. All too often a leveling phenomenon results where ev-eryone gets a little attention, but few receive the individual su-pervision they need. One man under supervision in California said his supervisor would not help him find a job. He continued:

> I mean, it's not really his fault because he got three hundred other guys. And he doesn't even know me. All he knows is my number is three seven such and such. All he knows is . . . if he wants to keep his job, all he got to do is have me come in once a week, piss in the bottle. As long as the bottle don't show no drugs in it, I can stay on the streets another week. First time the piss is not good, all he gotta do is send me to jail, that's it. He put my file back over there in "inactive" and that's it.

Such a system does little to protect public safety. It also does little to keep offenders out of trouble or to help them get their lives in order.

The problem is not the *concept* of probation, but the implemen-tation. If probation officers had the resources to properly super-vise and assist offenders, and if they understood their role as more than detecting violations, probation would be more effective.

INTENSIVE PROBATION

Intensive probation is a program that monitors the offender much more closely than traditional probation. Offenders in this program usually must contact their probation officer more than once per week, sometimes on a daily basis. While more expen-sive than ordinary probation, intensive probation permits the safe release of more serious offenders into the community. It costs an average of $2,912 per offender per year—much less than prison.

An intensive probation program in Georgia was designed for serious nonviolent offenders. It assigned two probation officers to twenty-five offenders and scheduled at least five face-to-face contacts each week. The total cost of a single probationer was about one-seventh the cost of operating a prison bed in Georgia. At the first evaluation, the failure rate was just 16 percent, with only 0.8 percent of the probationers committing a violent crime and none causing serious injury. Other intensive supervision programs have reported higher failure rates, but that appears due to the extremely close monitoring rather than heightened criminal activity.

Intensive probation is one of the most underutilized alternatives to incarceration. It is often the first program to be scaled back when spending is reduced, largely because it is considered "soft" on offenders. Most probation officers around the country currently are set up to fail. With each probation officer supervising more than 100 offenders, it is impossible to provide anything but the most minimal supervision. The solution should be more supervision, not less. If one considers the $22,000 annual expense of incarcerating a prisoner, the economics of probation become compelling. A single probation officer can intensively supervise anywhere from 20 to 30 offenders with enormous effect at a fraction of the cost of prison for each offender.

STUDIES SHOW THAT PAROLE WORKS

Two studies, one from Tennessee and the other from Iowa, show that parole does work. Despite all obstacles, the overwhelming majority of parolees do reintegrate into the community and sin no more.

For two years the Tennessee Sentencing Commission and the state's Bureau of Investigation tracked 3,793 prisoners released between July 1, 1989 and June 30, 1991. Most were parolees. Within two years of release, 24.7 percent were returned to prison for committing a new crime, 14.5 percent were reimprisoned for violating parole or probation rules, 14.3 percent were rearrested but not returned to prison, and nearly half of them, 46.5 percent, were not even arrested. . . .

In Iowa, for two years the parole board followed 1,039 parolees released between October 1, 1990 and April 1, 1991. Within two years of release, 324 parolees were reimprisoned for a "failure rate" of 31 percent. This means 69 percent succeeded in society and stayed out of prison.

Douglas Dennis, *Angolite*, March/April 1996.

Most prisoners are not released into complete freedom. They must first spend a number of years under the supervision of the department of parole. Though often misunderstood, parole serves a number of important functions. It allows the government to supervise offenders after release to help minimize the risk that they will commit new crimes. While in prison, it motivates offenders to follow the rules and take part in programs (successful completion of such programs usually impresses the parole board). People who are incarcerated with no possibility of parole have less incentive to take part in treatment programs and respect other inmates or guards.

Unfortunately, many parole officers see their jobs as limited to catching violators, rather than helping parolees deal with the problems involved in readjusting to life on the outside. When technical violations (e.g., missing a meeting) are observed, those on parole should be held accountable in some manner but not necessarily returned to prison. This is seldom done. For example, California parolees are supervised so tightly that most parolees end up right back behind bars—*even if they have not done anything criminal*. In 1991, nearly half of the people in California state prisons were there for technical violations of release, that is, violation of a condition of parole that did not itself warrant a new criminal charge. Most technical parole violations could be successfully and less expensively handled without reimprisoning the offender.

An alternative approach to parole would be to provide support services to increase the likelihood that the parolee will successfully make the transition from prisoner to citizen. In Virginia, when inmates are released from prison they are given $25 and a bus ticket. Unless the offender has a support network on the outside or has received training and treatment while in prison, such a release is a recipe for disaster. Virginians disappointed with supposed parolee misconduct have considered measures designed to eliminate parole altogether. They are not, however, considering an increase in parole supervision designed to help released inmates succeed. Such improved supervision can be a far superior means of ensuring the safety of the community at an affordable cost.

"We have abolished parole,
established the principle of truth-in-
sentencing, and increased . . . fivefold
the amount of time that violent
offenders will actually spend in jail."

STATES SHOULD ABOLISH PAROLE

George Allen

Republican George Allen was elected governor of Virginia in
1994. In the following viewpoint, Allen argues that Virginians'
outrage concerning high crime rates and criminals' early release
from prison prompted the state to overhaul its criminal justice
system, including eliminating parole and drastically increasing
offenders' prison terms. Allen cites data that show that the
longer an offender is incarcerated, the less likely the offender is
to commit another crime after release. Incarceration, Allen contends, is the most effective approach to prevent crime.

As you read, consider the following questions:

1. What was similar about the sentences given to first and
   repeat offenders, according to Allen?
2. What percentage of his or her sentence will a violent
   criminal serve under the new law, according to the author?
3. According to Allen, how much money will Virginia's law save
   its citizens?

George Allen, "The Courage of Our Convictions," Policy Review, Spring 1995. Reprinted by
permission of The Heritage Foundation.

On Father's Day 1986, Richmond Police Detective George Taylor stopped Wayne DeLong for a routine traffic violation. DeLong, recently released from prison after serving time for murder, shot and killed the policeman.

Leo Webb was a divinity student at Richmond's Virginia Union University who liked helping people. One of those he helped was a man named James Steele, on parole for a malicious wounding. One day in 1991, Steele entered the bakery where Webb worked part time, shot him to death, took his money, and went out partying.

Tragic as such stories are, what makes these two particularly disheartening is that both could have been easily prevented. Both killers, jailed earlier for violent crimes, spent only a fraction of their sentences in prison. We are now paying the dividends of a liberal justice system that refuses to take punishment seriously: Virginia witnessed a 28 percent increase in criminal violence from 1990 to 1995. Three out of every four violent crimes—murder, armed robbery, rape, assault—are now committed by repeat offenders.

INCARCERATION IS THE SOLUTION

This is why my administration pushed through legislation, which took effect on January 1, 1995, that will impose penalties for rape, murder, and armed robbery more than twice the national average for those crimes. We have abolished parole, established the principle of truth-in-sentencing, and increased as much as fivefold the amount of time that violent offenders will actually spend in jail. Experience vindicates what common sense has always told us: The only foolproof crime-prevention technique is incarceration.

Our new system is attempting to unravel 30 years of paper-tiger laws based on the questionable philosophy that people can change, criminals can be rehabilitated, and every violent criminal—even a murderer—deserves a second chance. The law in Virginia will prevent thousands of crimes, save lives, save money, and restore trust in the criminal justice system. Despite this, we now face entrenched opposition from liberals in the General Assembly, who hope to thwart reform by withholding funds to build the minimal number of prison facilities needed to house Virginia's most violent inmates.

A few weeks after taking office in January 1994, I created the Commission on Parole Abolition and Sentencing Reform. It was a bipartisan commission of prosecutors, judges, crime victims, law-enforcement officers, business leaders, and legal scholars.

William Barr, a former attorney general of the United States, and Richard Cullen, a former U.S. Attorney for the Eastern District of Virginia, co-chaired the commission. They had a daunting task.

I called for a special session of the General Assembly in September 1994 to focus the public's and the legislature's attention on this issue. I gave the commission six months to demonstrate the need for change, develop a detailed plan, and explain its costs and implementation.

We were quickly able to show why a complete overhaul was necessary. Convicted felons were serving about one-third of their sentences on average, and many served only one-sixth. Violent criminals were no exception. First-degree murderers were given average sentences of 35 years, but spent an average of only 10 years behind bars. Rapists were being sentenced to nine years and serving four. Armed robbers received sentences averaging 14 years and served only about four. (See chart 1.)

Amazingly, a prior conviction for a violent crime did not affect this phenomenon. Even murderers, rapists, and armed robbers who had already served time for similar offenses were receiving the same sentences and serving the same amount of time as first offenders.

Statewide, the violent crime rate had risen 28 percent in five years, even though the crime-prone age bracket (15 to 24 years) was shrinking. Criminologists widely regard trends in the size of this demographic group as the best predictor of criminal activity. Unfortunately for Virginians, the crime-prone-age population was expected to rise sharply in the state beginning in 1996—all the more reason to press forward with reform. The peak age for murder and armed robbery has been dropping steadily; by 1993, it stood at 18 years for both crimes. More than three-quarters of all violent criminals in the system in 1993 had prior convictions.

THE VIRGINIA PLAN

Only a multi-pronged approach can begin to turn these numbers around. Virginia's law means, first of all, eliminating discretionary parole, in which a parole board can release an offender after he has served only part of his sentence. In Virginia, this policy clearly was being abused: offenders received 30 days of good time for every 30 days they served—effectively cutting their sentences in half as soon as they came in the door.

But this is not all. We need to eliminate "good time" as well. In order to encourage good behavior among inmates and allow correctional officers to maintain order, the commission proposed a system of earned-sentence credits. This system would allow inmates to earn a maximum of 54 days per year—a dramatic reduction from the average of 300 days they had been given in the past.

Long before our bill became law, we held town meetings across the state to solicit advice from citizens, and discussed the plan's details with prosecutors, victims-rights groups, corrections experts, and criminologists. The need for more prison space became a primary concern. Even before I took office, Virginia was expected to double its prison population by the year 2005. The state was facing a shortfall of 7,100 prison beds by 1999. At the same time, opponents of the plan were already carping about too little spending on crime prevention and education and too much on building prisons.

CHART 1. REVOLVING-DOOR JUSTICE

Average Sentences vs. Actual Time Served by Criminals in Virginia prior to the 1995 law.

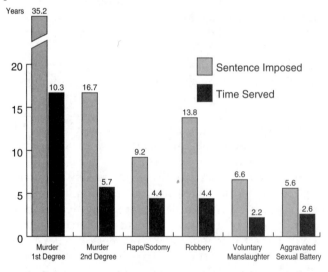

Source: Criminal Justice Research Center, cited in George Allen, *Policy Review*, Spring 1995.

Obviously, judges need some mechanism to guide their sentencing decisions. A system with no parole and no "good time" could not afford 70-year sentences for drug dealers or 150-year sentences for armed robbers. But how much do we increase the time served for violent offenders? Our commission found an answer by evaluating the relationship of recidivism to time

served and age of release. The data showed that the longer an offender remained behind bars, the less likely he is to commit another crime after finishing his sentence. Similarly, the older the
offender upon release, the less his propensity to commit more
crime. In fact, after 37 years of age, the likelihood of violent
crime drops dramatically.

Although preventing criminals from committing further acts
of violence was the primary goal, the increases had to reflect the
notion of retribution as well. We wanted Virginia to send a message to violent criminals: We will not tolerate violence, and if
you commit a violent crime, you will stay in prison until you're
too old to commit another one.

INCREASED PRISON TERMS

Virginia increased prison time for violent criminals as follows:
- 100 percent increase for first-time violent offenders.
- 125 percent for first-time murderers, rapists, and armed
  robbers.
- 300 percent for those with previous convictions for assault,
  burglary, or malicious wounding.
- 500 percent for those with previous convictions for murder, rape, or armed robbery.

To target the young violent offender, we counted comparable
juvenile offenses as felony convictions when determining a sentence. For example, if John Smith is found guilty in a juvenile
court of armed robbery at age 14, and was convicted of another
armed robbery at age 19, the sentencing guidelines call for a
500 percent increase in the time he normally would have served
under the old system.

By abolishing a bankrupt parole system, and by drastically reforming the "good time" credit provisions, Virginia courtrooms
are redefining what the truth-in-sentencing debate is really
about. Under our system, every inmate convicted of a violent
crime will serve a minimum of 85 percent of his or her sentence. Nationwide, criminals on average serve well below 50 percent of their sentences. There is simply no surer way for the state
to protect its citizens from society's most dangerous members.

SAVING LIVES AND MONEY

Had the law been in effect in 1986, it would have saved the life
of Detective Taylor. Had it been in effect in 1991, Leo Webb
would be alive today.

The most conservative estimates show that more than 4,300
felony crimes would have been prevented between 1986 and

1993 if the current system had been in place. That number is based on actual convictions—real cases, not projections.

Through the year 2005, the law will prevent at least 119,000 felonies, including 26,000 violent crimes. Because of those averted violent crimes, an estimated 475 lives will be saved, 3,700 women will be spared from rape, and more than 11,300 aggravated assaults will not be committed. As a result, citizens will save more than $2.7 billion in direct costs.

Back in September 1994, when it became clear that the legislation would pass with overwhelming support, some vocal opponents claimed that abolishing parole was a declaration of war on young black males. They demanded that the Commonwealth spend more money on prevention programs, and charged that, by focusing on punishment, we were merely catering to "white fear." Their arguments fell on deaf ears.

The crime prevented as a result of the law will benefit the African-American community—one-fifth of Virginia's population—more than any other group. Of the preventable murders that occurred between 1986 and 1993, about 65 percent involved black victims. For assaults during that same period, about 60 percent of the victims were black. Taylor and Webb were both African Americans.

Of all the crimes committed by recidivists during that same period, 60 percent would have been prevented if the current law had been in place. There is no other prevention program that can show even a fraction of this success. That is not to say that other prevention programs are not valid or important. However, it is clear that when it comes to violent offenders, incarceration is the most just and the most efficient. . . .

THE DEMAND FOR REFORM

The abolition of parole and establishment of truth-in-sentencing rules was the centerpiece of my campaign for governor in 1993. During that campaign, critics claimed my approach was too drastic and too costly. Pundits and politicians still doubt that Virginia can overhaul its entire criminal-justice system without breaking the bank. Those naysayers failed to hear the public's demand for change. The people of Virginia—particularly crime victims and their families—are tired of seeing criminals walk free after serving only a fraction of their sentences. Businessmen can't afford to watch deals collapse because potential clients are concerned about crime. Prosecutors and police are frustrated that their hard work often amounts to abbreviated prison stints for criminals.

In order to overturn the status quo approach to crime reduction, we listened to all those people and presented extensive research to show that what we had been doing was not working. Public safety is the primary responsibility of government. Without it, nothing else can succeed. Education, economic development, and health care all suffer when people feel threatened.

Virginians came together to formulate and implement this reform. We looked at what North Carolina, Texas, Florida, and the federal government had done in the area of sentencing reform. We borrowed some of the best aspects of those systems and avoided some of the mistakes they made. In the end, we did it the Virginia way.

The principle that guided this effort, and should guide policymakers in all issues, is honesty. Easy-release rules prevent judges and juries from preempting the community's judgment about the proper punishment for illegal conduct. Under the 1995 law, judges will not have to play guessing games when imposing sentences. Police officers will not have to see the same criminals out on the streets only a year after their last arrest. Criminals will know that they cannot beat the system. Crime victims and their families will finally see justice done. Virginia's citizens can now trust that their government is working to make this Commonwealth a safe place to live, to work, and to raise families.

> "What was initially viewed as a
> limited alternative to incarceration
> is now distinguished as an effective
> means of intervention."

ELECTRONIC MONITORING IS A SUCCESSFUL ALTERNATIVE

Darren Gowen

Electronic monitoring involves placing monitoring devices on the bodies and in the homes of criminal offenders so that they can be confined at home rather than in jails and prisons. In the following viewpoint, Darren Gowen describes the successful use of electronic monitoring in southern Mississippi. Gowen contends that electronic monitoring there has become an effective means of supervising pretrial defendants, probation violators, and other offenders. Gowen is a federal probation officer for the Southern District of Mississippi.

As you read, consider the following questions:

1. How many weekly contacts take place between an officer and an offender in the Mississippi program, according to Gowen?
2. In Gowen's opinion, what is the common argument made against the use of electronic monitoring? How does he respond to that argument?
3. According to the author, what was the failure rate in his district's electronic monitoring program?

Darren Gowen, "Electronic Monitoring in the Southern District of Mississippi," *Federal Probation*, vol. 59, no. 1, March 1995. (Notes and references in the original have been omitted.)

Nineteen ninety-four marked the first year that the United States Probation Office in the Southern District of Mississippi used electronic monitoring for home confinement cases. We originally expected that we would use this new program primarily to satisfy Federal sentencing guidelines in particular criminal cases. Beyond this, however, our expectations were not altogether clear. We also had some reservations about using electronic monitoring. Those who work in criminal justice are often quick to recall at least one catastrophe in which an electronically monitored offender "escapes" from home and 20 minutes later commits an armed robbery and kills a convenience store clerk. As probation officers, our overriding concern is community safety. Needless to say, our unfamiliarity with electronic monitoring only seemed to invoke numerous hypothetical catastrophic images.

However, these undesirable images quickly dissipated once our electronic monitoring program became firmly established. Once the various actors in the court arena, such as judges, prosecutors, defense attorneys, and probation officers, began recognizing its benefits, use of home confinement increased, particularly for pretrial defendants and court supervision violators. The resulting caseload expansion produced some interesting challenges in program administration and changed the nature of our overall supervision philosophy. This viewpoint describes some developmental aspects of our electronic monitoring program, including selection criteria, types of cases, supervision model, and offender demographics.

SELECTION CRITERIA

Initially, our selection criteria restricted participation in home confinement to a very select group of offenders (i.e., those with no violent, mental illness, or severe substance abuse history). With many new home confinement programs, as confidence with electronic monitoring technology grows, so does the acceptance of more high-risk offenders. Similarly, after several high-risk offenders slipped past our stringent entrance requirements— most successfully completing their term—we began seeing the positive behavioral impact electronic monitoring had on drug users and other "irresponsible" or noncompliant offenders.

The U. S. Probation Office in Southern Mississippi serves both probation and pretrial components in the court system. We originally began using electronic monitoring for only post-sentence cases. Later, we began recommending certain pretrial defendants for home curfew, home detention, or house arrest as a condition of bond. In our experience, defendants at the pre-trial stage are often more resistant to supervision than post-sentence offenders. It is not uncommon for pretrial defendants to display both attitudinal and behavioral hostility toward supervision efforts, possibly because of their new-found situation of being charged with a criminal offense. Although officers also observe these characteristics among the post-sentence population, they certainly appear more prevalent at the pretrial stage. Consequently, our experience supervising pretrial defendants on electronic monitoring led to our expanding the acceptance criteria for probationers and supervised releasees even more.

SUPERVISION VIOLATORS

After accumulating some degree of confidence in monitoring high-risk pretrial defendants, we next attempted to duplicate our efforts specifically with court supervision violators. According to current Federal community supervision imperatives, the selection of an intervention should be appropriate to the specific noncompliant behavior. Intervention should be timely, realistic, and progressive. Two distinct types of violators emerged as appropriate candidates for placement on home confinement:

1) *Substance abusers.* Those who test positive for alcohol or drugs, yet retain some semblance of employment and residential stability;

2) *Irresponsible offenders.* Those who fail to report, fail to complete community service, make false statements to the probation officer et al. (i.e., mainly technical violations).

Regarding the first category, if a person appears to have a good work history and stable living environment, he or she may be only a recreational drug or alcohol user. Of course, some severe drug and alcohol users are successful in maintaining a facade of normalcy in their lives, and we have had such individuals go on to complete a term of home confinement successfully. Incidentally, our district policy maintains a zero tolerance for drug use, so removal from the program is mandatory after testing positive for illegal substances only once.

The second category, "irresponsible offenders," is intended to depict those individuals who acquire repeated technical violations simply because of their own irresponsibility. Offenders who are difficult to "keep up with," as well as those who continually fail to comply with community service, restitution, or fine conditions, are good examples. Sometimes an offender may seem, at first, to fit this irresponsible profile but upon further investigation is found to be abusing alcohol or drugs, a characteristic of the first violator category.

With both types of violators, we quickly observed the incredible deterrent effect of the electronic ankle bracelet and the required adherence to a daily activity schedule. The bracelet, which transmits a signal for reception by a home monitoring unit, also serves as a constant reminder to the offender to comply with specified requirements. An approved daily activity schedule, which is used to allow the offender certain times of the day to be "in range" and "out of range" from the residence, is a product of an offender actually planning his or her life ahead of time. These two things alone can offer very effective intervention. Of course, if such intervention fails to achieve compliance, the threat of revocation as a backdrop to the home confinement alternative always serves as an additional motivator.

Using home confinement as a sanction for noncompliance requires modification of conditions by the court. Unlike much larger districts, such as Southern Florida, where petitioning the court for a modification takes a considerable length of time, in Southern Mississippi we can practically walk the paperwork through the necessary steps within 1 or 2 days (with offender consent).

OFFICER-OFFENDER CONTACT

The high number of personal contacts between officer and offender required by home confinement supervision sets the stage for a close rapport. Thanks to electronic technology, the officer receives daily, from the monitoring contractor, a facsimile consisting of reports, which summarize, among other things, offender departures from, and arrivals to, the residence. This high-precision information changes the communicable environment between officer and offender. For instance, should an offender arrive home 10–20 minutes late, the officer can confront the offender regarding this schedule aberration, usually within 24 hours. Such feedback on seemingly small violations helps to deter more serious ones.

Our limited experience with supervision violators on home confinement has demonstrated this new interpersonal environment helps regain compliance. Of course, officers should try other less intrusive sanctions before modifying conditions and proceeding with home confinement. But when increased contacts and other methods fail, the logical next step is home confinement, given certain residential and employment requirements.

Sometimes, however, home confinement might be the logical first step for sanctioning an offender. For instance, one of our supervised releasees tested positive for cocaine. He admitted using and indicated he used at night, particularly on weekends with his friends. The offender was already in drug aftercare. He resided with his mother and appeared to have a stable home situation. He also worked regularly for a construction company. The officer sought a modification for home confinement to restrict this person's activities outside of home and employment. On home confinement, the only place this offender went at night was to Alcoholics Anonymous meetings. With this particular individual, other types of sanctions, such as increased reporting, might have served only to identify additional violations rather than to correct his misbehavior. As it stood, the home confinement served as a logical first choice for effective correctional intervention.

Of course, not every supervision violator placed on home confinement succeeds. But it is important to understand that those who do succeed do so when less restrictive sanctions were largely ineffective and more restrictive sanctions (such as halfway house placement or revocation) might negate the responsibilities required to subsist successfully in the community—where most offenders eventually go.

PRETRANSFER AND PRERELEASE CASES

Home confinement might, in a very limited number of instances, enhance risk control over those offenders seeking transfer from a sentencing district to the district in which they previously resided. This tool might be suitable for those individuals having a poor track record on supervision—such as is common with some parole cases. The offender in question would have to agree to a modification of supervision conditions to include home confinement. The sentencing district court or the U.S. Parole Commission would also have to be agreeable. One interesting caveat to such a modification tied to transfer approval is that if an offender will agree to a term of monitoring, he or she most likely has legitimate intentions in relocating.

A modification to add home confinement as a supervision condition might serve some limited purpose for offenders seeking approval for their release plan to the community. For example, in our district a Choctaw Indian convicted of a sex offense was restricted, as a supervision condition, from the Indian reservation where the victim resided. This condition had a definite purpose. But the offender had no family ties, or means of support, off the reservation. To prevent this individual from defiantly residing on the reservation anyway, regardless of any court order, we opted to allow him limited access to the reservation with a modification for home confinement. The offender, while still in custody, agreed to a term of home confinement. The sentencing court agreed to allow the defendant access to the reservation, residing in a different community (location) than the victim.

Monitoring Drug Offenders

A wide-area monitoring system might replace prison for those given the minimum sentences now imposed for drug offenses unmarred by violence. Certainly the monitoring of drug offenders would hinder any further drug transactions. Drug dealers could develop new delivery scenarios, but the tracking system would make this less convenient.

Further, to counter possible drug abuse by some offenders, the locator could be equipped with a broad-based tool for monitoring vital signs such as pulse rate and blood pressure.

Joseph Hoshen, Jim Sennott, and Max Winkler, IEEE *Spectrum*, February 1995.

The obvious point of this discussion on pretransfer and prerelease cases is that home confinement with electronic monitoring is a very useful, flexible tool to ensure compliance for those cases presenting unique supervision challenges. The above example illustrates our propensity for operating within the enhanced supervision framework for case planning—ensuring the adherence to court orders, controlling risk to the community, and offering correctional treatment.

The Supervision Model

Unlike larger districts serving high population metropolitan areas, Southern Mississippi has a largely rural population. This presents some unique supervision challenges. Offenders residing in rural areas are supervised by general supervision officers assigned to that specific geographical area. A home confinement coordinator is on call to the monitoring contractor in the case of alerts. Thus, instead of one officer maintaining a full caseload of home confinement cases, each officer in the supervision unit has several of these specialized cases. Supervision officers rotate on-call duty—handling alerts from the monitoring center—on weekends.

According to local policy, a minimum of two personal contacts between officer and offender are required each week. Usually, offenders report to the probation office once a week; officers make at least one surprise personal visit, at home or elsewhere, each week. Collateral contacts with employers and significant others are made monthly. These contacts verify compliance with both electronic monitoring/home confinement rules as well as other supervision conditions. Office visits are used for urine collections, checking the transmitter or bracelet on the offender's ankle, and making schedule changes for the remainder of the week. Home visits are necessary, not only to check the offender's living situation, but to check the monitoring unit as well. Since the monitoring unit and electronic bracelet only verify an offender's presence at home, collateral visits are necessary to verify the offender's whereabouts when "out of range" of the residence.

Special equipment enables us to enhance surveillance of electronically monitored offenders, especially when they are away from (i.e., out of range of) home. Officers use a hand-held, portable receiver for detecting the presence of a transmitter's signal, the condition of the transmitter battery, and whether a tamper condition exists. This device allows the officer, for instance, to drive anonymously by the building where an offender is working and immediately know if he or she is inside, without even getting out of the car.

Home confinement with electronic monitoring requires increased field supervision, which represents an increased risk to officer safety. Fortunately, our use of two-way mobile radios, cellular phones, pagers, portable receivers, bullet-resistant vests, nonlethal devices (CapStun), and firearms assists our officers in meeting these responsibilities safely.

When responding to an alert requiring a home visit during off-duty hours, policy dictates that two officers respond. Supervisor approval must be obtained before dispatching to an offender's residence. We also request assistance from local law enforcement when personally responding to alerts at night.

OFFENDER DEMOGRAPHICS

A common argument made against the use of electronic monitoring as an alternative to incarceration is that the selection requirements are potentially discriminatory against minorities and particularly those in lower socioeconomic classes. Common sense tells one that a wealthy offender, restricted to a luxurious home, is not being punished or sanctioned to the same extent as the individual who lives in a housing project. Unfortunately—as many practitioners will attest—many of those at the bottom of the socioeconomic stratum enjoy better living conditions in custody. During our first year of electronic monitoring we detected no programmatical bias favoring white-collar offenders.

Although no data were collected on income or other socioeconomic phenomena, my unscientific observations were that Southern Mississippi's proclivity to place higher-risk pretrial defendants and supervision violators in the electronic monitoring program had a balancing effect on representation along the socioeconomic continuum.

As to racial composition, the general population in Southern Mississippi, as well as our total supervision caseload (both probation and pretrial), could be characterized as an almost equal distribution between blacks and whites. The racial composition of home confinement cases in 1994, then, is not surprising: 60 percent of the total caseload was white, 36 percent black, and 4 percent Indian. As to gender, 22 percent were female.

Out of our annual cumulative total caseload of 49, 4 cases (8 percent) failed. Two of these failures were for unauthorized leave—both were Bureau of Prisons inmates. The third failure was for not adhering to home confinement and other probation conditions (not paying utility bills and not maintaining employment). The fourth was a pretrial defendant who tested positive for cocaine. Although a majority of the total caseload consisted of male participants, only one of the four failures was male.

EXPANDING ELECTRONIC MONITORING

We began our first year of electronic monitoring with limited expectations about its use and with very stringent entrance requirements. As the year went along, we began accepting much higher risk cases with excellent results—not the catastrophes we first imagined. This led to our expanding the use of home confinement to supervision violators and also to selected pretransfer and prerelease cases where closer monitoring might be useful in risk management.

Common perceptions about electronic monitoring held by our staff, as well as by the judges in our district, have changed tremendously. What was initially viewed as a limited alternative to incarceration is now distinguished as an effective means of intervention. Our home confinement supervision model has been adapted to suit a largely rural populace, which requires that supervision case assignments be dispersed among many general supervision officers rather than to just one home confinement specialist. We hope our experience with electronic monitoring can be of benefit to others in similarly sized districts who want to expand the use of this new technology in their own supervision efforts.

| "We have seen little theoretical or empirical support to justify the rush to [electronic monitoring]."

ELECTRONIC MONITORING MAY NOT BE SUCCESSFUL

Ronald Corbett and Gary T. Marx

In the following viewpoint, Ronald Corbett and Gary T. Marx argue that local electronic monitoring (EM) programs may not succeed. Corbett and Marx contend that widespread acceptance of EM stems from the persistence of various "technofallacies"—false beliefs regarding the value and effectiveness of technological solutions for social problems. They maintain that some law enforcement agencies are highly receptive to EM despite evidence of its failings, including breakdowns caused by environmental conditions and computer, power, and telephone failures. EM should not be automatically embraced simply because it is a new technology, the authors assert. Corbett is the deputy commissioner of the Massachusetts Department of Probation. Marx is a sociology professor at the University of Colorado in Boulder.

As you read, consider the following questions:

1. According to Corbett and Marx, why are agency administrators fond of innovations?
2. What examples of past corrections panaceas do the authors offer?
3. In the authors' opinion, what limitations in telephone service could inhibit electronic monitoring?

Excerpted from Ronald Corbett and Gary T. Marx, "Critique: No Soul in the New Machine: Technofallacies in the Electronic Monitoring Movement," *Justice Quarterly*, vol. 8, no. 3, (September 1991). Reprinted with permission of the Academy of Criminal Justice Sciences.

It's a remarkable piece of apparatus.

Opening line, *The Penal Colony*, by Franz Kafka

S ince its legendary inception in the mind of a New Mexico judge inspired by *Spiderman* comics, the use of electronic monitoring as a correctional tool has grown in a manner most often described as "explosive." From very isolated use in 1984, the use of electronic monitoring (hereafter EM) has expanded to at least 33 states, with a threefold increase during 1988 alone.

Although hardly a mature industry, EM has attracted a growing number of manufacturers now totaling at least 14. For the last several years, exhibition areas at the annual conference of the American Probation and Parole Association have been occupied almost entirely by vendors of new technology, most of it EM equipment.

Clearly, EM has arrived on the correctional scene and has drawn much attention. Significant research findings regarding its impact recently have begun to come in. These studies have intensified the debate about the proper place of EM in criminal justice. In this viewpoint we locate EM in the context of broader societal developments regarding surveillance, and we argue that unfortunately it has fallen prey to a series of technofallacies which undermine practice. Viewing the current electronic monitoring frenzy from the perspective of several decades of observing and participating in the correctional process, we have [Hall of Fame baseball catcher] Yogi Berra's sense that "it's deja vu all over again," as yet another panacea is offered to criminal justice without adequate thought or preparation.

We address both academic and practitioner audiences. The former will recognize the sociological perspectives of unintended consequences, irony, and paradox as applied to a new area. We hope that the latter—those who develop and administer policy—will gain from this presentation by seeing that innovations never stand alone and that avoidance of the fallacies identified here can mean improved practice. . . .

TECHNO-FALLACIES OF ELECTRONIC SALVATION

New public policies are based partly on politics and interests, partly on empirical assessment, and partly on values. Unfortunately, wisdom too often plays only a modest role.

EM must be approached cautiously, or the stampeding herd may fall off the cliff. Before technical solutions such as monitoring are implemented, it is important to examine the broader cultural climate, the rationales for action, and the empirical and value assumptions on which they are based. Policy analysts must offer not only theories, concepts, methods, and data, but also—one hopes—wisdom. Part of this wisdom consists of being able to identify and question the structure of tacit assumptions that undergird action.

In the analysis of new surveillance technologies, Gary Marx identifies a number of "tarnished silver bullet techno-fallacies" that characterize many recent efforts to use technology to deal with social issues. Some of these apply to the case at hand. In critiquing the EM movement, the following discussion draws on and expands this more general framework. We discuss several such fallacies. . . .

New Is Not Necessarily Good

The fallacy of novelty. This fallacy entails the assumption that new means are invariably better than the old. Decisions are often based on newness rather than on data suggesting that the new will work or that the old has failed. The symbolism of wanting to appear up-to-date is important.

The fallacy of novelty is related to a "vanguard" fallacy: "If the big guys are doing it, it must be good." Smaller organizations copy the actions of the larger or more prestigious organizations in an effort to appear modern.

The field of corrections often has been accused of being in constant thrall to fads and panaceas. Technofix attitudes unfortunately have become the knee-jerk response of our society to complex issues whose causes are social, not technical. In a theme with solid roots in American history, newness is equated too quickly with goodness. New technology is inherently attractive to an industrial society. It's risky to be against new technology, however mysterious its operations or recondite its underlying engineering. Technical innovation becomes synonymous with progress. To be opposed to new technology is to be a heretic, to be old-fashioned, backwards, resistant to change, regressive, out of step. Ian Reinecke observes sardonically, "To fall behind in the great technorace is to demonstrate a pathetic unwillingness to change with the times, to invite universal ridicule, and to write a recipe for economic disaster."

Agency administrators become fond of the new and the original as a matter of careerism and survival. Fast-track reputations are more likely to be built on introducing new programs than on maintaining the old; few professionals want to be regarded as caretakers. Invitations to speak at conferences, media coverage, job offers, and, most significantly, the availability of grant money depend on the implementation of novel approaches. Questions about the fit of the innovation with the agency's mission and goals or about the existence of empirical support for the innovation will be considered mere details in the face of these forces. This point leads directly to our next fallacy.

IGNORING NEGATIVE EVIDENCE

The fallacy of intuitive appeal or surface plausibility. This entails the adoption of a policy because "it sure seems as if it would work." The emphasis is on commonsense "real-world" experience and a dash of wish fulfillment in approaching new programs. In this ahistorical and anti-empirical world, evaluative research has little currency.

The models for rational policy development taught in schools of public administration advance the notion that in the domain of social policy, research and evaluation determine policy. Unfortunately, these models usually bear little resemblance to actual occurrences in corrections practice. James O. Finckenauer refers to a tendency for agencies to ignore evidence of program failure if the ideological "spin" is right. Todd R. Clear and Patricia Hardyman speak of a rush to embrace intensive probation supervision [IPS] when the evidence supporting such adoption is "weak." Michael Tonry and Richard Will cite administrators who proliferate programs and believe in their efficacy, even in the absence of careful evaluations. They note that "in a field (community corrections) . . . in which few rigorous evaluations have been conducted, the persuasive force of conventional but untested wisdom is great."

Enthusiasm for EM programs runs high, even when data that call them into question are available. Joan M. Petersilia's three-county random-assignment experiment involving EM in California found the following: "The highest technical violation and arrest rate occurred in the Electronic Monitoring Program in Los Angeles. About 35% of participants in the program had a technical violation, and 35% an arrest, after six months." Probation with EM was found to result in rearrest rates identical to those of offenders under regular supervision.

STUDIES SHOW NO BENEFITS

An Indianapolis study released in 1990 compared the effectiveness of EM with that of human monitoring. No significant differences were found between the two methods. The study revealed, however, that nearly 44 percent of all participants "sneaked out" on the monitoring.

In Billie Irwin's report on the use of EM in the Georgia IPS program, she concludes that it was a failure and that it seemed to exacerbate recidivism rates. Dennis J. Palumbo, Mary Clifford, and Zoann Snyder-Joy report that in an Arizona EM study concentrating on cost-effectiveness, the evidence suggests that EM did not reduce and might very well increase overall correctional costs due to net widening.

Just as innovations are promoted without regard to supporting data, so can traditional approaches be abandoned casually with a lack of evidence. In the late 1970s and early 1980s it became the conventional wisdom that rehabilitation was a failure and that programs aimed at reforming offenders were bankrupt. EM and other "get tough" approaches to community corrections flourished in this environment, as the emphasis shifted toward punishment and deterrence.

No Benefits

A review sponsored by U.S. Department of Justice on the effectiveness of [electronic monitoring] devices concluded that they do not save money, free jail beds or deter crime. The three-year survey of the monitoring system's use in Oklahoma concluded in 1990 that the devices were useful only for a narrow segment of defendants and prisoners and, even in those cases, had no meaningful impact.

Defendants wearing the tracking cuffs were no more likely to appear for court than other offenders, the study showed, nor did the device seem to affect recidivism rates.

Ken Ellingwood and Geoff Boucher, *Los Angeles Times*, May 28, 1996.

Again, it is remarkable how little this conventional wisdom was supported by the available research. James M. Byrne, in an overview of intensive supervision programming, inveighs against systems that blindly negate or minimize the importance of treatment interventions and overestimate the impact of control-oriented interventions such as EM. Petersilia's methodologically rigorous study reports, as its only positive finding, that lower recidivism rates were found "among those ISP offenders who were fortunate enough to receive some rehabilitative programming." In a major study of the effects of a sanctioning approach versus a treatment approach in reducing recidivism, D.A. Andrews and his colleagues found that across 80 different studies, criminal sanctioning without the provision of rehabilitative services did not work and that only programs incorporating principles of rehabilitation reduced recidivism significantly. They conclude, "There is a reasonably solid clinical and research basis for the political reaffirmation of rehabilitation."

THE DOWNSIDE OF INNOVATION

The fallacy of the free lunch or painless dentistry. This fallacy involves the belief that there are programs which will return only good results without any offsetting losses. It ignores the existence of low-visibility or longer-range collateral costs, and fails to recognize that any format or structure both channels and excludes.

In the making of public policy, new ideas all too often drive out old ideas, irrespective of their merit. New programs draw attention and resources away from the traditional efforts. This situation can entail significant opportunity costs. Personnel and other resources will be allocated to the innovation, often starving (or undernourishing) existing programs. Over time, the conventional ways of doing business may suffer from choked-off budgets and the retention of less competent staff members who have been excluded from the new, high-priority program. Such persons also may be angry about not being included in the new programs.

Eventually this "Gresham"-style effect may develop a self-fulfilling quality. Whatever the merit of conventional programs, they become defenseless against the drain of resources into the innovation. Conversely, the innovation, whatever its merits, is provided with an introduction under the most favorable circumstances (ample start-up funds, generous publicity, an elite, hand-picked staff). This makes for an unrealistic test of its potential under normal non-"halo" conditions.

The EM movement illustrates these dynamics nicely. Clear and his colleagues, in their review of three intensive supervision projects, discuss the "secondary place" taken by treatment efforts when control is emphasized. Irwin, in discussing the use of EM in Georgia, observes that although the technology makes the control function easier, "at the same time [it] may make more difficult the part of the job that involves the motivation of offenders and gaining their cooperation." Palumbo and colleagues conclude that because the program is sold on the basis of its capacity to control offenders, treatment becomes at best an "add-on": "Under these conditions, there is likely to be little if any real treatment provided.". . .

A CORRECTIONS FAD

The fallacy of ignoring the recent past. For the case at hand, this fallacy involves denying the possibility that EM might be just another corrections fad. Of course this characterizes nontechnical reforms as well. Yet whether from genuine enthusiasm or as a political strategy, those caught up in the excitement and the high stakes of promoting a reform often wear historical blinders. They do so at their peril.

The intense interest in EM has all the earmarks of a fad—broad media attention, quick, widespread adoption, rapid expansion and diversification of the product. Even a superficial familiarity with the recent history of community corrections should encourage a skeptical, or at least a go-slow, approach.

The history of the last 20 years of community corrections is punctuated at about five-year intervals by the appearance of new "panaceas," typically arriving suddenly and attracting enormous attention. The bad news is that they tend to disappear just as quickly. Examples include pretrial diversion in the late 1960s, mandatory sentencing in the mid-1970s, and intensive probation supervision (IPS) in the early 1980s. Their trajectory has been roughly similar: great early enthusiasm, widespread adoption, less-than-positive evaluations followed by disillusionment, and finally downscaling or elimination and receptiveness to the next panacea. . . .

TECHNICAL FAILURES

The fallacy of the 100% accurate or fail-safe system. The glamour surrounding sophisticated electronic technology may lead the uncritical to assume that its results are invariably reliable. In their enthusiasm vendors and program entrepreneurs may fail to acknowledge the technology's weaknesses. As an assessment by Joseph Papy and Richard Nimer of EM in Florida put it, "The technology has proven both reliable and unreliable." It may break or fail to work under certain conditions. The technology is also applied and interpreted by humans, with the possibility for errors and corruption.

There are many examples of technical failures: transmissions can be blocked or distorted by environmental conditions such as lightning, proximity to an FM radio station, the metal in mylar wallpaper and trailer walls, some house construction materials, and water in a waterbed or bathtub (with some early versions participants even got electrical shocks while bathing). Poor telephone lines, wiring and equipment may transmit signals that cannot be accurately read. Power, telephone and computer failures may make it appear that a violation has occurred when it hasn't, or the reverse. The quality of telephone service required for confidence in the voice verification system is not available in many places. Those monitoring the system to report violations can be compromised and with private contractors there may be less accountability than in the public sector. Of course in the adversarial context many participants will seek ways to neutralize the system and to exploit its ambiguities (at least four in ten do so according to research by Terry L. Bauman and Robert I. Mendelsohn). . . .

RISKING DAMAGE

In Kafka's short story *The Penal Colony*, a correctional officer and his superior develop a complicated new machine capable of inflicting horrible mortal punishment on inmates. In the end, the officer who argued so proudly for the new technology is horrifically consumed by it. We don't suggest that anything like this will necessarily happen in corrections, but it is clear that innovations which are not thought out carefully and offered honestly and modestly run the risk of doing great damage. So far we have seen little theoretical or empirical support to justify the rush to EM.

| "The success of Delancey Street has
created an enormous demand for
similar programs in other areas
throughout the world."

DRUG TREATMENT IS AN EFFECTIVE ALTERNATIVE

Mimi Silbert and Stephanie Muller, interviewed by Julie Fretzin

In the following viewpoint, excerpted from an interview by Julie Fretzin, Mimi Silbert and Stephanie Muller describe the success of rehabilitation programs at the Delancey Street private treatment centers. Silbert and Muller contend that the centers' residents learn how to live without drugs and criminal activity by receiving self-help therapy, learning marketable skills, and helping newer residents. Silbert is the cofounder and president of the Delancey Street Foundation in San Francisco. Muller, a former drug addict, is a Delancey Street resident and supervisor of its Training Institute. Fretzin is a former marketing director of Friends of Creation Spirituality, an organization in Oakland, California.

As you read, consider the following questions:

1. What "unique feature" does Silbert credit for Delancey Street's success?
2. On what grounds does Silbert oppose incarcerating offenders?
3. According to Muller, how do residents learn the basic concepts of Delancey Street?

From "Crime and Transformation," an interview of Mimi Silbert and Stephanie Muller, by Julie Fretzin, *Creation Spirituality*, Fall 1994. Reprinted by permission of Julie Fretzin.

In reaction to the continuous assault of images of violent crime on television and in newspapers, Americans in unprecedented numbers are crying out for "get tough on crime" measures. Crime, according to current polls, is the nation's number-one concern. In a wave of hysterical fear, citizens who are unwilling to pay for the cost of improving schools are voting to spend unbelievable amounts of money to build more prisons and increase prison terms.

Such a gulf of separation exists between the fearful public and its image of those who perpetrate crime, that the criminal is seen as beyond hope, beyond help. In contrast, Dr. Mimi Silbert, president of the Delancey Street Foundation, sees the situation of many criminals as similar to the residents of the Boston immigrant neighborhood she grew up in. They are people who have never learned how to live in the American system.

DELANCEY'S GROWING SUCCESS

Cited as the most successful self-help organization in the nation, Delancey Street was named after the New York neighborhood where immigrant families at the turn of the century crowded together and helped each other move up to a better life. Delancey Street began in 1971 in San Francisco, when Silbert teamed up with ex-felon John Maher, who introduced the idea of a rehabilitation program run "by ex-cons, for ex-cons." The concept was that addicts and ex-cons are best equipped to understand the experience and see through the excuses of those in similar positions.

From its beginning, Delancey Street has operated without public assistance or professional staff. A variety of businesses have been created at Delancey Street over the years to support the organization and provide opportunities for residents to learn marketable skills. Today Delancey Street nets over $6 million from businesses that include Christmas tree sales, moving and hauling, furniture design, printing, and catering.

In 1989, Delancey Street opened its new headquarters at the Embarcadero Triangle on San Francisco's waterfront. Ninety percent of the construction work on this magnificent Italian-style 350,000-square-foot structure was done by Delancey Street residents with help and instruction from members of local trade unions. Five hundred residents live in the 177 apartments arranged in a complex which is designed to resemble a college campus. Additionally, five hundred residents live in the four other Delancey Street facilities that have been established in Los Angeles; Brewster, New York; Greensboro, North Carolina; and San Juan Pueblo, New Mexico.

The success of Delancey Street has created an enormous demand for similar programs in other areas throughout the world. In response, Delancey Street has developed a Training Institute so that the valuable lessons learned from their experience can be passed on. In the elegant but cozy Delancey Street Restaurant, which is run by the residents, I interviewed Mimi Silbert along with resident Stephanie Muller, who supervises the Training Institute.

TURNING AROUND CRIMINALS' ENERGY

Mimi, what originally led you to get involved in this kind of work?

Silbert: The people here feel to me like the people I grew up with. I have always felt like, with just a quick flip of the penny, they could be me. I know this sounds crazy, but I like the energy of criminals. They do everything backwards, but I always thought, "What if we could flip that energy totally around?" You see, these people haven't given up. Or rather, their version of giving up is not to die, but to keep clawing and spitting and being destructive and self-destructive and violent. But still, they keep coming. And it just seemed to me that if you could take that and turn it in the opposite direction, there would be such a potential life-force.

When I left my old neighborhood, I didn't leave behind my liking for poor, trapped, angry people. I had many versions of how I thought I wanted to turn that energy around. At first, I thought I was going to teach English because reading authors like Dostoyevsky just made me so much stronger and more committed. And I was convinced that if I could just get the right books to people, I could make a difference. I spent a semester trying to teach, and I found out it just doesn't work that way. It was probably a silly notion anyway. But now, we teach those things at Delancey Street.

What do you feel are the most important ingredients in making the Delancey Street program work?

Silbert: One unique feature of Delancey Street, that makes it so hard to replicate, is that you have to be willing to completely take a risk on the people who are the problem, to make them the solution. And we do that one hundred percent. Our residents typically have everything wrong with them. They've literally failed at everything. They're violent. They've been victims of child abuse. Most of them have been in gangs. They've been in prison time after time. But the idea is to truly live together like an extended family, with the kind of support and discipline that will teach us everything we need to know to make it. There is no solution but our own people. Occasionally someone comes in and tutors a class or helps us buy the right kind of lettuce for the restaurant, but for the most part, it's set up so that the residents do it themselves. People just have to stretch beyond anything anybody ever thought they were capable of doing.

COST-EFFECTIVE TREATMENT CUTS COCAINE USE

A study of cocaine control strategies by RAND researchers C. Peter Rydell and Susan S. Everingham finds that treatment is seven times more cost-effective than law enforcement in reducing cocaine consumption. . . .

Treatment is so cost-effective because it targets cocaine consumption directly. Some 80% of heavy users stay off drugs while in treatment, and about 13% of treated addicts kick the habit— some permanently, others temporarily. By contrast, supply control methods such as law enforcement and drug seizure are relatively indirect and highly expensive.

Gene Koretz, *Business Week*, August 14, 1995.

Another important aspect of Delancey Street is that, although we're a self-help organization, our real focus is more on learning to help someone else. Our organization is based on the concept of: "Each one teach one." People learn to be givers and doers rather than receivers. As soon as you learn something, you have to teach it. As soon as someone comes in who is newer than you, you have to help that person. All the rest of us are just at higher points on this mountain that we're all trying to climb. And I'm always trying to explain to our residents that, once we're all holding hands climbing this mountain, it doesn't really matter where you are. The person at the top may keep tugging to pull up, but if people further down keep tugging down, we all go down. So we're always focused on the newest people. . . .

THE SAME PHILOSOPHY

How has the philosophy of Delancey Street evolved as the program has grown?

Muller: The philosophy, remarkably, has stayed exactly the same from the minute it opened. The difference now is that we're into the second or third generation of drug addict/violent prison people. Whereas twenty years ago a lot of our people had parents who were working people, now their parents are dope fiends and in prison, and sometimes their grandparents are in prison. That's a major change among the people. It takes a lot longer to peel away the layers and find out what kind of little person is in there.

Silbert: The general public would rather see these people

locked up for the rest of their lives. But I interned as a prison psychologist, and it was clear to me that this system of punishment doesn't work. The people who wind up in prison are given everything, all paid for by the taxpayer, and they're responsible for nothing. And then we wonder why, when they come out, they're no different.

This is why we decided to move ahead with our Training Institute. Such a cluster of horrors are happening to people at the bottom of our society, that it's no longer right not to try to make it possible to duplicate what we do here on a large scale. So the Training Institute is our newest, most exciting child.

TRAINING TREATMENT PROVIDERS

How did you go about launching the Training Institute?

Muller: We had received over ten thousand letters from people all over the world who wanted us to start a Delancey Street in their community. Because we weren't able to hire people or buy property in other places, we thought the best idea would be to bring people here to learn all the psychological underpinnings of Delancey Street, the different structures, how we set it up. We sort of submerge them into day-to-day life at Delancey Street, explaining it as we go along. We don't set up any kind of false group sessions or mock classes. People participate in whatever we're doing to begin with, the different training schools that the residents go to, the encounter sessions that they attend. We explain what's happening as we go along. People in the Training Institute eat breakfast, lunch and dinner with the residents. They live in dorm situations. In this way, people absorb what it is that we do and apply it to what they're already doing. We sometimes keep in contact and give advice.

How do you communicate the intangible aspects of what goes on here?

Muller: The basic concepts that Delancey Street is based on— ethics and morals and integrity and commitment—these things take time to learn. And you learn them by living them. That's why Delancey Street is long term. You can't buy these concepts. You can't learn them on a video. It takes living it. People want a quick fix. They say, "If we build a great big, pretty building like this, will it cure people?" Well, no, it won't. It involves commitment, and it involves making people accountable for things.

COURAGE AND MIRACLES

What is involved in building the trust that enables people to change?

Silbert: It's not that things are not difficult at Delancey Street. It's not that you don't get betrayed every five minutes. You do, because that's what our residents are best at doing. But I have seen this unbelievable courage in our people in the face of all odds against them. When you're self-destructive, it's obsessive. It's compulsive. It talks to you all the time. It tells you, "Don't go for this, don't do that. This is bullshit." Everything inside them is telling them, "Go to the left, go to the left, go to the left." And I stand there and I say, "Trust me, come to the right." And they don't know how to do it. They feel stupid and awkward; they feel like they're going to lose everything if they give up the only world they know. They're never going to be able to make it in the other world. And then they'll have no world.

Imagine a forty-year-old person who has killed a few people and had a few people killed and just been nothing but destructive his whole life. He's evil incarnate, and in his mind everyone else is, too. And you see that person in front of you just slowly get wide-eyed like a child and begin to believe, begin to trust, begin to feel. This certainly takes well over a year. It takes well over a couple of years for that first real, decent feeling to come. But little miracles like that happen to people every day here. And to me, that is the thing I am so in love with that no matter how bad it gets—and it gets bad—I just keep coming back for more.

Do you believe that the principles that work at Delancey Street can be applied more broadly in our society? ...

Silbert: The same concepts that we work with here can be applied to any population, the idea of people supporting one another, but not supporting each other's craziness. Self-destruction by its nature is self-centered. It goes in the wrong direction. We work with people at the absolute bottom, and if our people can break through, I really believe that anybody and everybody can.

| "The real-world fact is that many treatment programs are simply not effective."

DRUG TREATMENT IS NOT AN EFFECTIVE ALTERNATIVE

William J. Bennett and John P. Walters

In the following viewpoint, former federal drug policy directors William J. Bennett and John P. Walters argue that the ineffectiveness of many drug treatment programs makes them a less appealing option than incarcerating offenders or stanching the supply of drugs. Bennett and Walters criticize the federal government's drug treatment bureaucracy and its misdistribution of funds. The authors also contend that drug courts that mandate treatment instead of prison are unsuitable for long-term, hardcore addicts. Bennett is codirector of Empower America, a conservative think tank in Washington, D.C. Walters is president of the New Citizenship Project in Washington, D.C.

As you read, consider the following questions:

1. How many addicts receive treatment annually, according to Bennett and Walters?
2. In Bennett and Walters's opinion, what group could benefit from properly run drug courts?
3. According to the authors, what is the likely fate of cocaine addicts?

William J. Bennett and John P. Walters, "A Record of Failure in Drug Treatment," *Washington Times*, February 8, 1995. Reprinted by permission of The Washington Times Corporation.

> [W]e should deal with the drug problem in a far more heads-up manner than we are now with two things. Number one, treatment on demand without delay. . . . The second thing we ought to do is find an alternative for first-time drug offenders.
>
> —Bill Clinton, address at Georgetown University,
> December 12, 1991.

Today's addicts are the most visible casualties of both the permissive culture and the drug fad of the late 1960's, 70's, and early 80's. These addicts have moved up in the ranks from casual users. They are largely aging, never married, and predominantly male. Most commit crimes—including selling drugs—as a means of income to purchase drugs. They are also largely concentrated among blacks and live in our inner cities. While these addicts constitute the single largest demand for heroin and cocaine in the United States, they also use a variety of other drugs (particularly marijuana) and alcohol.

The overwhelming reaction to this problem has been a call for more drug treatment. "Treatment on demand" is the preferred weapon of many in the drug fight. In fact, many liberals have argued the rational and humane response to drug addiction is to shift resources from drug enforcement and supply reduction to drug treatment.

There are a number of very sophisticated and very effective drug treatment programs (many of which we visited), including very modest ones sponsored by churches and using variants of the 12-step method. These are often every bit as effective as much more expensive and elaborate programs. But the typical discussion of drug treatment in the press and by the government reflects a dangerous ignorance of the most basic facts.

TREATMENT FAILURE

First, the government treatment bureaucracy is manifestly wasteful and ineffective. From fiscal 1988 to fiscal 1994, federal drug treatment spending almost tripled. At the same time, however, the number of treatment slots remained virtually unchanged and the estimated number of people treated actually declined by 145,000. Why? As with much of government, it is because the bureaucracies have consumed more and more of the resources, leaving less and less for services.

Bureaucratic waste and inefficiency aside, the number of addicts served per year, measured in terms of persons served per year, is equivalent to more than half the total estimated number of cocaine and heroin addicts. Clearly, when given the chance, the bulk of these programs are not that successful.

A substantial number of addicts have attended several treatment programs. The real-world fact is that many treatment programs are simply not effective. In addition, federal treatment funds continue to be distributed largely on the basis of population, even though we know that addicts are concentrated in our major cities. And there has been no effort to ensure that addicts are placed in appropriate programs. Today, outpatient treatment slots predominate when most experts argue that the only reasonable hope of successfully treating today's hard-core addicts is to place them in long-term, residential treatment. Bush Administration efforts to make programs accountable—to cut off support to those that did not produce results, and match resources with the need—were not enacted by the Democratic leadership in Congress. And the Clinton Administration has abandoned all such efforts.

Drug Courts

In the 1994 crime bill large sums were offered for drug courts. These provisions were highlighted by liberals who announced that they were being "smart and tough." The model, and essentially the justification, for this funding was the Miami Drug Court and Attorney General Janet Reno's personal involvement with it as a prosecutor. But in August 1994, as the crime bill fight was near its peak, the *Miami Herald* published a lengthy report raising serious questions about the effectiveness of the program. In particular, the program established to divert first- and second-time drug offenders into treatment instead of prison was being used by robbers and burglars to serve as little as 45 days. And in December 1994 the *Herald* reported that the chief judge overseeing the Miami Drug Court ordered an audit of the entire program, expressing alarm that it "had no mechanism to measure whether it was succeeding." A central flaw in the rush to embrace drug courts as a major answer to addiction and crime is that a very large number of addicted offenders today are long-term, hard-core addicts who are poorly suited for diversion programs. Drug courts, properly run, may hold promise for treating young addicts. But young addicts are not the primary problem.

Misleading Studies

In 1994, two groups of studies were released that purport to demonstrate the effectiveness of drug treatment and its superior cost-effectiveness to all other categories of drug-enforcement and supply control. One, funded by the California Department of Alcohol and Drug Programs, received attention for its conclusion that treatment "averages [a] $7 return for every dollar invested." But it included both alcohol and drug addiction and was thus too broad to be enlightening in regard to the cost-effectiveness of treating cocaine, and particularly crack, addiction—the most destructive addiction threat today. None of the sympathetic news reports noted that such "benefits-to-society-for-every-dollar-invested" studies for expenditures on prisons and jails have produced estimates as high as 17-to-1.

FEDERAL DRUG TREATMENT SPENDING AND PERSONS TREATED

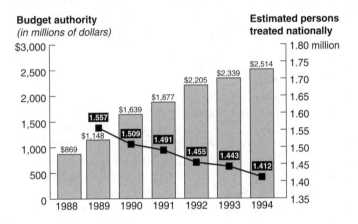

Source: National Drug Control Strategy, 1994.

A second, widely-reported study, was funded in part by the White House drug office, and conducted by the RAND Corp. It was entitled "Controlling Cocaine," and concluded that "treatment is seven times more cost effective in reducing cocaine consumption than the best supply control program." Most of the press reports on the release of this study failed to mention that even Clinton Administration drug office officials participating in the release distanced themselves from the reliability of the methods RAND used to measure the effectiveness of supply control programs. And to our knowledge none of the press reports explained what the study actually found in regard to the effectiveness of programs treating cocaine addicts.

In reviewing all forms of cocaine treatment, RAND found that 20 percent of addicts continue using drugs while in treatment and only 13.2 percent of the cocaine addicts treated reduce their drug use below weekly or more frequent use (what

RAND defined as "heavy use") during the year following their treatment. Overall, RAND reported, only "6 percent of heavy users leave heavy use each year [i.e., to something less than heavy use, not to be equated with no use]. About two-thirds of that outflow is apparently due to existing treatment programs . . . [and] one-third of the total annual outflow from heavy use is estimated to be due to unassisted desistance from heavy use."

THE REALITIES OF DRUGS

In other words, overall, cocaine treatment is only 4 percent effective in reducing heavy use and only 2 percent more effective in reducing heavy use than no treatment at all. Needless to say, if the effectiveness of cocaine treatment were measured in terms of the percentage of addicts who stopped using cocaine altogether and for good, these numbers would be much, much smaller.

While we should continue to support treatment programs, we need to face the harsh reality of cocaine and crack addiction: most addicts are likely to die from the effects of their addiction, sometime in their 40's, if not earlier. This is yet one more compelling reason why preventing casual drug use by young people—the first step on the path to addiction—is so important.

As long as the drug problem is discussed in terms of treatment vs. enforcement or supply vs. demand, it will remain fundamentally misguided. These dogmatic positions are at odds with both reality and common sense. An effective drug policy should begin with this assumption: as long as young people and those who receive treatment reside in communities where the supply of dangerous, addictive drugs remains plentiful—i.e., where there is de facto legalization—prevention and particularly treatment efforts will be severely undercut, and for purposes of national policy, ineffective.

PERIODICAL BIBLIOGRAPHY

The following articles have been selected to supplement the diverse views presented in this chapter. Addresses are provided for periodicals not indexed in the *Readers' Guide to Periodical Literature*, the *Alternative Press Index*, the *Social Sciences Index*, or the *Index to Legal Periodicals and Books*.

Michael P. Brown and Preston Elrod	"Electronic House Arrest: An Examination of Citizen Attitudes," *Crime and Delinquency*, vol. 41, no. 3, July 1995.
Karen De Witt	"Crowded Jails Spur New Look at Punishment," *New York Times*, December 25, 1995.
Thomas Falater	"Future Pen: The Prisons of Tomorrow," *Prison Life*, July/August 1995. Available from PO Box 537, Stone Ridge, NY 12484.
Joseph Hoshen, Jim Sennott, and Max Winkler	"Keeping Tabs on Criminals," *IEEE Spectrum*, February 1995. Available from 345 E. 47th St., New York, NY 10017.
Eric Lotke	"Sex Offenders: Does Treatment Work?" *Research Update*, April 1996. Available from National Center on Institutions and Alternatives, 635 Slaters Ln., Suite G-100, Alexandria, VA 22314.
Patricia Loveless	"Home Incarceration with Electronic Monitoring: Myths and Realities," *American Jails*, January/February 1994. Available from American Jail Association, 2053 Day Rd., Suite 100, Hagerstown, MD 21740-9795.
Greg D. Richardson	"Parole No More?" *Justice Report*, Fall 1995. Available from PO Box 16069, Washington, DC 20041-6069.
Sheryl Stolberg	"Study Shows Drug Abuse Programs Are Cost-Effective," *Los Angeles Times*, August 29, 1994. Available from Reprints, Times Mirror Square, Los Angeles, CA 90053.
Jeffrey Tauber	"Treating Drug-Using Offenders Through Sanctions, Incentives," *Corrections Today*, February 1994.

For Further Discussion

Chapter 1

1. Pete du Pont argues that prison labor's "competitive pressures on individual firms or local labor" is not a sufficient reason to restrict prison work. Do you agree with the author that prison labor should be pursued even though private businesses and workers could be harmed? Why or why not?

2. Michael Corsentino describes the harsh conditions that prison chain gang workers endure. In your opinion, is the use of inmate chain gangs inhumane? Does the fact that many inmates volunteer for chain gangs affect your answer in any way? Explain.

Chapter 2

1. The *Washington Times* argues that the annual expense of incarcerating a criminal is a fraction of the cost of the crimes that the criminal would otherwise commit if he or she were free. Jon Marc Taylor maintains that the prison system's high costs have not reduced crime or benefited inmates. How do the authors support their arguments? Whose argument is stronger, and why?

2. The Council on Crime in America, citing several studies detailing the economic loss from personal and violent crimes, contends that the financial impact of crime justifies the cost of building and operating prisons. What criticisms does the National Criminal Justice Commission have concerning prison expenditures? In your opinion, do these criticisms effectively counter the argument of the Council on Crime in America? Explain your answer.

3. Michael K. Block and Steven J. Twist argue that prisons are the key to protecting the public and that keeping Americans safe from criminals is a higher priority than funding social programs. Do you agree with the authors' arguments? Why or why not?

Chapter 3

1. Francis T. Murphy contends that rehabilitation will not likely succeed in a prison environment where personal safety, health, and humane treatment are compromised. What specific measures do you think prisons could adopt to make rehabilitation succeed?

2. C. Askari Kweli is a maximum-security inmate in California. In

your opinion, does this fact make his allegations of abuse by prison guards more or less believable? Explain your answer.

3. Those who support the use of "supermaximum" security argue that the most violent inmates do not deserve the privileges that other prisoners enjoy. Opponents contend that such treatment is unfair and does nothing to help prisoners. What privileges, if any, do you think should be afforded to supermaximum security inmates? Defend your answer.

4. Robert James Bidinotto contends that many prisoners enjoy a variety of "creature comforts." Jon Marc Taylor disagrees, calling Bidinotto's viewpoint propaganda. Which author presents his case most persuasively? Explain, using examples from the viewpoints.

CHAPTER 4

1. William M. DiMascio describes a number of intermediate sanctions for offenders. Consider each sanction and rank them according to what you believe is their effectiveness. Explain your reasoning.

2. William J. Bennett and John P. Walters are former federal drug policy directors. Mimi Silbert and Stephanie Muller supervise a drug treatment facility. How are the authors' backgrounds evident in their views of drug users? Which of these viewpoints is more convincing, and why? Does knowing the authors' backgrounds influence your assessment of their arguments? If so, in what way?

ORGANIZATIONS TO CONTACT

The editors have compiled the following list of organizations concerned with the issues debated in this book. The descriptions are derived from materials provided by the organizations. All have publications or information available for interested readers. The list was compiled on the date of publication of the present volume; names, addresses, phone and fax numbers, and e-mail and Internet addresses may change. Be aware that many organizations take several weeks or longer to respond to inquiries, so allow as much time as possible.

American Civil Liberties Union (ACLU)
National Prison Project
1875 Connecticut Ave. NW, Suite 410, Washington, DC 20009
(202) 234-4830 • fax: (202) 234-4890

Formed in 1972, the project serves as a national resource center and litigates cases to strengthen and protect adult and juvenile offenders' Eighth Amendment rights. It opposes electronic monitoring of offenders and the privatization of prisons. The project publishes the quarterly *National Prison Project Journal* and various booklets.

American Correctional Association (ACA)
4380 Forbes Blvd., Lanham, MD 20706-4322
(301) 918-1800 • fax: (301) 918-1900

The ACA is committed to improving national and international correctional policy and to promoting the professional development of those working in the field of corrections. It offers a variety of books and correspondence courses on corrections and criminal justice and publishes the bimonthly magazine *Corrections Today.*

Bureau of Prisons
320 First St. NW, Washington, DC 20534
Internet: http://www.bop.gov

The bureau works to protect society by confining offenders in the controlled environments of prison and community-based facilities. It believes in providing work and other self-improvement opportunities within these facilities to assist offenders in becoming law-abiding citizens. The bureau publishes the book *The State of the Bureau.*

Campaign for an Effective Crime Policy
918 F St. NW, Suite 505, Washington, DC 20004
(202) 628-1903 • fax: (202) 628-1091

Coordinated by the Sentencing Project, the campaign's purpose is to promote information, ideas, discussion, and debate about criminal justice policy and to move sentencing policy toward alternative sentencing. The campaign's core document is *A Call for a Rational Debate on Crime and Punishment.*

Center for Alternative Sentencing and Employment Services (CASES)

346 Broadway, 8th Fl., New York, NY 10013
(212) 732-0076 • fax: (212) 571-0292
e-mail: cases1@ix.netcom.com

CASES seeks to end what it views as the overuse of incarceration as a response to crime. It operates two alternative-sentence programs in New York City: the Court Employment Project, which provides intensive supervision and services for felony offenders, and the Community Service Sentencing Project, which works with repeat misdemeanor offenders. The center advocates in court for such offenders' admission into its programs. CASES publishes various program brochures.

Citizens United for Rehabilitation of Errants (CURE)

11094D Lee Hwy., Suite 200, Fairfax, VA 22030
(703) 352-4788 • fax: (703) 591-2505

CURE is an organization that works to reduce crime through the reform of the criminal justice system. Its goals are to ensure that prisons are used only for individuals who absolutely require incarceration and that prisoners have all the resources necessary for rehabilitation. CURE publishes the monthly newsletter *Citizens Agenda* and various position papers.

The Enterprise Prison Institute (EPI)

1899 L St. NW, Suite 500, Washington, DC 20036
(202) 466-7001 • fax: (202) 466-7002

Formed in April 1996, the EPI is a bipartisan research and educational organization dedicated to helping policymakers and criminal justice professionals improve the management of the criminal justice and prison systems. The EPI has published the survey "Prison Industries Challenges and Strategies" and a prison industries briefing paper.

The Fortune Society

39 W. 19th St., 7th Fl., New York, NY 10011
(212) 206-7070 • fax: (212) 366-6323

The society is an organization of ex-offenders and others interested in penal reform. It is dedicated to educating the public about prisons, criminal justice issues, and the root causes of crime. The society also works to help former prisoners break the cycle of crime and incarceration. Its publications include the quarterly *Fortune News*.

The Heritage Foundation

214 Massachusetts Ave. NE, Washington, DC 20002
(202) 546-4400 • fax: (202) 546-0904

The Heritage Foundation is a conservative public policy research institute. It is a proponent of limited government and advocates tougher sentencing and the construction of more prisons. The foundation publishes articles on a variety of public policy issues in its Backgrounder series and in its quarterly journal *Policy Review*.

Justice Fellowship

PO Box 16069, Washington, DC 20041-6069
(703) 904-7312 • fax: (703) 478-9679

The Justice Fellowship is a national criminal justice reform organization that advocates victims' rights, alternatives to prison, and community involvement in the criminal justice system. It aims to make the criminal justice system more consistent with biblical teachings on justice. It publishes the brochures *A Case for Alternatives to Prison*, *A Case for Prison Industries*, *A Case for Victims' Rights*, and *Beyond Crime and Punishment: Restorative Justice*, as well as the quarterly newsletter *Justice Report*.

Law Enforcement Alliance of America (LEAA)

7700 Leesburg Pike, Suite 421, Falls Church, VA 22043
(703) 847-2677 • fax: (703) 556-6485

LEAA is a nonprofit, nonpartisan advocacy organization made up of law enforcement professionals, crime victims, and concerned citizens dedicated to making America safer from crime. It provides assistance to law enforcement professionals, promotes victims' rights over criminals' rights, supports criminal justice reform that targets violent criminals, and opposes gun control. It publishes the quarterly magazine *LEAA Advocate*, which periodically addresses correctional issues.

National Association of Chiefs of Police (NACP)

3801 Biscayne Blvd., Miami, FL 33137
(305) 573-0070 • fax: (305) 573-9819

NACP is a nonprofit educational organization of police chiefs and command law enforcement officers. It provides consultation and research services in all phases of police activity. NACP publishes the bimonthly magazine the *Chief of Police* as well as an annual spring survey of command law enforcement officers.

National Center on Institutions and Alternatives (NCIA)

635 Slaters Lane, Suite G-100, Alexandria, VA 22314
(703) 684-0373 • fax: (703) 684-6037
Internet: http//www.ncianet.org/ncia

NCIA is a criminal justice foundation that encourages community-based alternatives to prison that are more effective in providing education, training, and personal skills required for the rehabilitation of nonviolent offenders. The center advocates doubling "good conduct" credit for the early release of nonviolent first-time offenders in the federal system to make room for violent offenders. NCIA publications include the report "An Analysis of Juvenile Homicides: Where They Occur and the Effectiveness of Adult Court Intervention" and the books *The Real War on Crime* and *Search and Destroy: African American Males in the Criminal Justice System*.

Prisoners' Rights Union (PRU)

PO Box 1019, Sacramento, CA 95812-1019

(916) 441-4214 • fax: (916) 441-4297

The PRU's primary goal is to educate California prisoners about their civil rights and to ensure human rights for all prisoners. It publishes the *California State Prisoner's Handbook* and the quarterly newspaper *California Prisoner*, which reports on the current status of legislative and judicial decisions that affect the lives of prisoners and their families.

The Rand Corporation

1700 Main St., PO Box 2138, Santa Monica, CA 90407-2138

(310) 393-0411 • fax: (310) 393-4818

Internet: http://www.rand.org

The Rand Corporation is an independent nonprofit organization engaged in research on national security issues and the public welfare. It conducts its work with support from federal, state, and local governments and from foundations and other philanthropic sources. Its publications include the book *Prison vs. Probation: Implications for Crime and Offender Recidivism* and the report "Three Strikes and You're Out: Estimated Benefits and Costs of California's New Mandatory-Sentencing Law."

The Sentencing Project

918 F St. NW, Suite 501, Washington, DC 20004

(202) 628-0871 • fax: (202) 628-1091

The project seeks to provide public defenders and other public officials with information on establishing and improving alternative sentencing programs that provide convicted persons with positive and constructive options to incarceration. It promotes increased public understanding of the sentencing process and alternative sentencing programs. It publishes the reports "Americans Behind Bars: A Comparison of International Rates of Incarceration," "Americans Behind Bars: One Year Later," and "Young Black Men and the Criminal Justice System: A Growing National Problem."

BIBLIOGRAPHY OF BOOKS

Allen J. Beck and Lawrence A. Greenfeld — *Violent Offenders in State Prison: Sentences and Time Served.* Washington, DC: U.S. Department of Justice, Office of Justice Programs, Bureau of Justice Statistics, 1995.

Nils Christie — *Crime Control as Industry: Towards Gulags, Western Style.* New York: Routledge, 1995.

Ernest L. Cowles and Thomas C. Castellano — *"Boot Camp" Drug Treatment and Aftercare Intervention: An Evaluation Review.* Washington, DC: National Institute of Justice, 1995.

Roberta C. Cronin — *Boot Camps for Adults and Juvenile Offenders: An Overview and Update.* Washington, DC: National Institute of Justice, 1994.

Steven R. Donziger — *The Real War on Crime: The Report of the National Criminal Justice Commission.* New York: HarperCollins, 1996.

R. Antony Duff and David Garland, eds. — *A Reader on Punishment.* New York: Oxford University Press, 1994.

Timothy J. Flanagan, ed. — *Long-Term Imprisonment: Policy, Science, and Correctional Practice.* Thousand Oaks, CA: Sage, 1995.

Lois G. Forer — *A Rage to Punish: The Unintended Consequences of Mandatory Sentencing.* New York: Norton, 1994.

Mansfield B. Frazier — *From Behind the Wall: Commentary on Crime, Punishment, Race, and the Underclass by a Prison Inmate.* New York: Paragon House, 1995.

Daniel Glaser — *Preparing Convicts for Law-Abiding Lives: The Pioneering Penology of Richard A. McGee.* Albany: State University of New York Press, 1995.

Alan T. Harland — *Choosing Correctional Options That Work.* Thousand Oaks, CA: Sage, 1996.

John Irwin and James Austin — *It's About Time: America's Imprisonment Binge.* Belmont, CA: Wadsworth, 1994.

Robert Johnson — *Hard Time: Understanding and Reforming the Prison.* 2nd ed. Belmont, CA: Wadsworth, 1996.

Josine Junger-Tas — *Alternatives to Prison Sentences—Experiences and Developments.* Lanham, MD: American Correctional Association, 1994.

Roy D. King and Kathleen McDermott	*The State of Our Prisons.* New York: Oxford University Press, 1995.
Norval Morris, ed.	*Between Prison and Probation: Intermediate Punishments in a Rational Sentencing System.* New York: Oxford University Press, 1990.
Norval Morris and David Rothman, eds.	*The Oxford History of Prisons: The Practice of Punishment in Western Society.* New York: Oxford University Press, 1995.
Office of Juvenile Justice and Delinquency Prevention	*Unlocking the Doors for Status Offenders: The State of the States.* Washington, DC: U.S. Government Printing Office, 1995.
Jeffrey Reiman	*The Rich Get Richer and the Poor Get Prison.* Boston: Allyn and Bacon, 1995.
Wilbert Rideau and Ron Wikberg	*Life Sentences: Rage and Survival Behind Bars.* New York: Random House, 1992.
John W. Roberts, ed.	*Escaping Prison Myths: Selected Topics in the History of Federal Corrections.* Washington, DC: American University Press, 1994.
Elihu Rosenblatt, ed.	*Criminal Injustice: Confronting the Prison Crisis.* Boston: South End Press, 1996.
William L. Selke	*Prisons in Crisis.* Bloomington: Indiana University Press, 1993.
George E. Sexton	*Work in American Prisons: Joint Ventures with the Private Sector.* Washington, DC: U.S. Department of Justice, 1995.
David Shichor	*Punishment for Profit: Private Prisons/Public Concerns.* Thousand Oaks, CA: Sage, 1995.
David Shichor	*Three Strikes and You're Out.* Thousand Oaks, CA: Sage, 1996.
Matthew Silberman	*A World of Violence: Corrections in America.* Belmont, CA: Wadsworth, 1995.
John Simmons, Marshall Cohen, Joshua Cohen, and Charles Beitz	*Punishment: A Philosophy and Public Affairs Reader.* Princeton, NJ: Princeton University Press, 1994.
J.R. Sparks, Anthony Bottoms, and Will Hay	*Prisons and the Problem of Order.* New York: Oxford University Press, 1996.
Michael Tonry	*Sentencing Reform in Overcrowded Times.* New York: Oxford University Press, 1997.

U.S. Congress, House Committee on the Judiciary, Subcommittee on Crime and Criminal Justice

Correcting Revolving Door Justice: New Approaches to Recidivism. Washington, DC: U.S. Government Printing Office, 1995.

Jerome Washington

Iron House: Stories from the Yard. Fort Bragg, CA: QED Press, 1994.

Michael Welch

Corrections: A Critical Approach. New York: McGraw-Hill, 1996.

Tamasak Wicharaya

Simple Theory, Hard Reality: The Impact of Sentencing Reforms on Courts, Prisons, and Crime. Albany: State University of New York Press, 1995.

INDEX